VICTOR UNITS OF THE COLD WAR

SERIES EDITOR: TONY HOLMES

OSPREY COMBAT AIRCRAFT • 88

VICTOR UNITS OF THE COLD WAR

ANDREW BROOKES

OSPREY
PUBLISHING

Front Cover

The Blue Steel missile had been designed to travel at speeds up to Mach 3 and deliver a megaton warhead over a 150 statute mile range. A special high test peroxide (storable)/kerosene rocket motor named the Stentor was built by Armstrong Siddeley at Coventry to power the weapon. The Stentor's main combustion chamber produced 16,000 lbs of thrust, which was supplemented by a secondary chamber that added an additional 4000 lbs of thrust. The main combustion chamber drove the missile up to 70,000 ft, where it levelled off. The main chamber then cut out and the secondary took over, this being enough in the rarefied air to sustain a speed of Mach 2.5. Marconi Elliot at Rochester built the inertia navigator which required no radio signals to go about its business.

Wittering Wing Victor B 2Rs became operational with the weapon at low level in 1964. Modifications that were made to individual Blue Steels to allow them to perform the low level mission were not extensive, with the main difference being that the Stentor's two combustion chambers now fired together. However, release range was dramatically reduced to 25-30 miles at low level, and when it was at release point the Victor had to climb sufficiently to give the missile adequate room to fall away before it fired.

Of the 57 Blue Steel stand-off missiles bought by the RAF, four were specifically for in-service proof firings by Bomber Command after the weapon's entry into service. The first of these proof firings, codenamed Operation *Fresno*, took place from Victor B 2R XH673 of No 100 Sqn flying at 1000 ft asl and 350 knots IAS over the Aberporth Range, in Wales, on 27 May 1966. Blue Steel is shown here falling freely over Cardigan Bay to clear the aircraft before the liquid-fuelled rocket motor fired. Two seconds later the missile controls unlocked and it zoomed to 17,000 ft, at which point the Stentor cut out. The missile knew its distance out and its distance off from the target, and it tried to fly the most direct route in between. Directional control was on the 'twist and steer' principle by which each turn was begun by rolling with the inboard ailerons on the rear mounted delta wing, and then maintained by increasing lift on the small delta-shaped foreplanes. The inertial navigator was forever looking for a particular dive angle to the target, and when it got there, down went the missile to simulate penetrating the defences. On 27 May 1966, the Blue Steel's 'components functioned properly and it impacted within 1000 yards of the 25 nautical mile range target' (*Cover artwork by Gareth Hector using a model supplied by* Milviz)

For Simon

First published in Great Britain in 2011 by Osprey Publishing
Midland House, West Way, Botley, Oxford, OX2 0PH
44-02 23rd St, Suite 219, Long Island City, NY 11101, USA
Email: info@ospreypublishing.com
Osprey Publishing is part of the Osprey Group.

© 2011 Osprey Publishing Limited

A CIP catalogue record for this book is available from the British Library

ISBN: 978 1 84908 339 3
Ebook ISBN: 978 1 84908 340 9

Edited by Tony Holmes
Page design by Tony Truscott
Cover artwork by Gareth Hector
Aircraft profiles by Chris Davey
Index by Michael Forder
Originated by PDQ Digital Media Solutions, Suffolk, UK
Printed in China through Bookbuilders

12 13 14 15 16   11 10 9 8 7 6 5 4 3 2

The Woodland Trust
Osprey Publishing is supporting the Woodland Trust, the UK's leading woodland conservation charity, by funding the dedication of trees.

www.ospreypublishing.com

CONTENTS

VICTOR EMERGENT

Duringworld War 2 Handley Page was best known for its four-engined HP 57 Halifax bomber. In 1943 the company resumed work on a private venture swept-wing tailless research aircraft designed before the war to overcome the problems of drag and centre of gravity displacement caused by heavy tail armament. Aircraft, especially bombers, get attacked mainly from the rear, but conventional bombers such as the Halifax could not carry large rear turrets because that would make them tail-heavy. Neither could the turret operate effectively from the mid-position because the tail and fin got in the way, but if the tail was removed, the aircraft would not need such a large fuselage and the turret could be positioned near the centre of gravity with an uninterrupted arc of fire.

Out of all this good stuff came the two-seat twin-pusher HP 75, which first flew in August 1943. The little aircraft had swept wings with a fin and rudder on each tip, and it was christened 'Manx' because Manx cats have no tails. Although it was a World War 2 concept with no reference to high Mach number research, the Manx pointed Handley Page in the direction of a tailless bomber weighing 70 tons.

The Avro Lincoln replaced the Lancaster and Halifax as the RAF's big bomber in 1945. When English Electric tendered successfully for their Canberra twin Avon-engined jet bomber to replace the Mosquito, Sir Frederick Handley Page was so confident that a similar replacement would be needed for the Lincoln that he issued a confidential memorandum on 14 June 1945 requesting an immediate investigation into two classes of bomber – one was of 100,000-lb all-up weight with four Avon-sized turbojets (or two of twice that size), and the other was a 60,000-lb twin Avon creation, but both were to make use of the experience gained with the tailless Manx.

The bulk of the initial research work fell on the firm's Research Engineer, Godfrey Lee. He was responsible for future projects, and as the

The diminutive two-seat HP 75 Manx tailless twin-pusher flew for about 18 hours in 1943 before terrible vibration caused parts of the airframe to fall off in flight

Germans had led the field in high speed aeronautical research up to then, Lee was sent as the company's representative on a mission to study the Luftwaffe's tailless aircraft projects in October 1945. The 32-year-old Lee spent his time talking mostly to research engineers and aerodynamicists at the Völkenrode experimental establishment near Brunswick and in the old university town of Göttingen. 'It was there we found out the true story of what wing sweep could do for you, namely that you could have a sensible thickness/chord ratio of 10-12 per cent and still fly at Mach 0.8 upwards without serious drag rise', Lee recalled.

On his return, he put forward a proposal for an aircraft powered by four Avon jet engines with a 122-ft span, a wing area of 2100 sq ft, an aspect ratio of seven and a wing loading of 43 lb/sq ft to carry a 10,000-lb bomb at 520 knots over a still air range of 5000 miles. This swept wing creation had wing tips that curved upwards until they were vertical. Christened the HP 80, it was in keeping with current RAF thinking.

The higher a bomber flew, the harder it would be to catch, and the faster it travelled, the less time it would be exposed to detection and attack. In those days, experts believed that Mach 1 was a barrier that man crossed at his peril, so if the RAF went for an attacker that could fly in the stratosphere at the brink of the sonic barrier, it would force an opponent to cross and re-cross this hazard as he tried to intercept.

Thus the idea of a sleek HP 80 stripped of turrets and armour appealed to the RAF, who issued Specification B 35/46 on 24 January 1947 which called for a 'day and night medium range bomber landplane capable of carrying a 10,000-lb bomb (the weight of the first British atom bomb called Blue Danube) to a target 1500 nautical miles from a base which may be anywhere in the world'. Cruising speed was to be 500 knots (575 mph, which equated to Mach 0.873 in the stratosphere), and the aircraft had to be capable of exceeding an altitude of 50,000 ft. B 35/46 preferred that the aircraft had no fewer than four and not more than six engines, and stipulated that it must be operable from existing bomber airfields. 'Catapult or trolley launching is not acceptable, nor is arrester gear for landing'.

To meet this requirement, Handley Page came up with a wing tapered from an inboard section of maximum 53 degrees sweepback to minimise frontal drag and compressibility, out to a tip of moderate 22 degrees sweep to preclude the chances of tip stall. In between was an intermediate section of around 35 degrees to blend the two extremities together. The result was a 100 ft-span wing of around 2000 sq ft area in which three changes of sweep, or 'kinks', were equally spaced. This then was the crescent wing, combining a swept-back thick wing and an unswept wing on one aerofoil with the added advantage that, by varying wing thickness along the sweep, it was possible to maintain a constant critical Mach number from root to tip.

The aircraft could not have reached 50,000 ft with less wing area, and there was enough depth at the wing root to accommodate the engines. No one would dream of fitting engine intakes into 53 degrees of sweep today. Nearly 1000 lb of thrust would be found to be blanked off the outboard engines of the production HP 80 when standing still at take-off power because the air flow concentrated at the outer corner of the intake. The aircraft had to roll well down the runway before the missing thrust was gathered back. Handley Page did not realise this in 1947, and very encouraging results had been obtained at Göttingen with such an arrangement.

'Perhaps we were the only firm brave enough or daft enough to do it', said Lee, but in 1947 the USAF B-52 solution of engines in underwing pods meant induced drag plus a larger fin and rudders to cope with asymmetric flight when the aim was to achieve the cleanest possible profile drag. If drag was caused by the airflow meeting the large wing root, it made sense to let some of it pass through the engines that fitted snugly into the six-foot-deep HP 80 wing root.

Sir Fred never liked the vertical wing tip fins, believing that shock waves might form on one and not the other, so they were deleted in early 1948, allowing Lee to increase wing span to 110 ft and to add a rear fin, with rudder and tailplane on top. Most of the two-stage sweep tailplane was elevator, and eventually the tailplane span was only 11 inches shorter than that of the Hawker Hunter mainplane it resembled.

It is open to debate whether the HP 80 planform should more accurately be termed a scimitar or a cusp rather than a crescent, but this wing was undoubtedly the most efficient high-subsonic wing on any drawing board in 1947. The compound sweep concept was not entirely new, for Dipl Ing R E Kosin, Arado's chief aerodynamicist, had come up with the same answer when called upon to produce a high speed wing for the Arado Ar 234 V16 jet bomber. It is popularly believed that Lee discovered this wing on his visit to Germany in 1945, but this is incorrect. He never visited any aircraft firm apart from that of the Horten Brothers at Göttingen, who built the Gotha Go 229 – the world's first pure flying wing jet bomber – and he certainly had never heard of the Arado design. 'The one real concept we got out of the German visit was that sweep was a good thing', Lee later recalled, 'and the crescent wing on the HP 80 was evolved by ourselves at Handley Page. It did not arise from anything Arado or anybody else did'.

Six designs were submitted to meet Spec B 35/46, the most advanced of which were the HP 80 and the delta wing Avro 698 Vulcan. As officialdom could not decide between them, the Ministry ordered both and then added the Vickers Valiant as an insurance measure.

The HP 80 was built in three major sub-assemblies – front, combined centre and rear and tail cone. At the front was the H2S navigation and bombing radar scanner and prone visual bombing station. Next came the crew pressure cabin, where the original design envisaged a first pilot's seat on the port side staggered slightly forward of the co-pilot's on the starboard. The two navigators had forward-facing seats behind the co-pilot, while slightly ahead of them on the port side sat the radio and electronics operator. In an emergency they were all to be ejected in a capsule which would float down under a large parachute. When that proved too difficult, the nose was attached permanently to the fuselage by four large bolts where the explosive attachments were to have gone. The flightdeck was altered so that ejection seats could be fitted for the pilots, but the rear crew of three, now facing backwards in line abreast, were expected to bail out through the entrance door on the port side.

The main thing that rankled at Handley Page throughout the war was the way the Halifax was always overshadowed by the Lancaster, which

Blue Danube was the first operational atomic bomb produced by Britain. The warrant officer standing to the right of the weapon gives some idea of the size of the 10,000-lb bomb

they ascribed to the fact that the Lancaster was capable of adaptation to carry far greater bomb loads, and therefore always stole the limelight. Although the primary load of the HP 80 was to be Blue Danube, Assistant Chief Designer Charles Joy remembers that they strove to give their HP 80 a bomb capacity double that of the Lancaster, and in this endeavour they were greatly assisted by the crescent wing.

Whereas the dimensions of the Valiant and the Avro delta bomb-bays were somewhat restricted by great spars, the centre wing structure of the HP 80 ended at about 30 per cent chord and therefore, because of the high sweep, the centre wing spar box was well forward of the aircraft's centre of gravity where it crossed the fuselage. This meant that the bomb-bay had only to carry the weight of bombs or other military loads through four equally spaced fore and aft girders attached at intervals to heavy box-section frames.

At a time when the Boeing B-52A bomber was being designed around a military load of 34,000 lbs, the HP 80, despite being less than half the B-52's gross weight, had a bomb-bay that was theoretically big enough to accommodate no fewer than 48 1000-lb bombs. 'It was another very important feature', said Godfrey Lee. 'There was so much that fitted together correctly in this aeroplane'.

The man who took the first HP 80 prototype, WB771, into the air was Chief Test Pilot Sqn Ldr Hedley George Hazelden. 'Hazel' had joined Handley Page in April 1947 at the age of 32, and within two months he was called into Chief Designer Reggie Stafford's office and told of the firm's latest challenge – a bomber they thought would be capable of 500 knots, 50,000 ft and a range of 5000 miles. 'If you can find out how to build it', he told Stafford, 'I'll find out how to fly it'.

On 24 December 1952, while the rest of the world was cranking up the Yuletide spirit, 'Hazel', together with flight test observer Ian Bennett, climbed aboard the silver HP 80. WB771, a flying shell weighing around 95,000 lbs, did two low circuits with the undercarriage down to test the ground effect of the combination of swept wing and high tail, before landing after a 17-minute flight. On 2 January 1953 the Air Ministry officially announced that the aircraft had been named 'Victor'.

A standard Handley Page test pilot's trick was to approach their Radlett airfield at 6000 ft, wait until the runway threshold had passed under the nose, then close the throttle, open the airbrakes and land with concrete to spare. It was great stuff, helped by the fact that there never was such an aircraft as the Victor with a comparable array of stall warnings. The first indication was the illumination of the coefficient of lift lights accompanied by automatic lowering of the nose flaps, provided they were selected to AUTO. Around this speed some peculiar noises – likened to an elephant trumpeting – emanated from the nostril air intakes as the flow broke down. Buffeting started perceptibly some 30 to 40 knots

below the flap-operating speed, increasing in violence down to the stall proper. Yet as soon as the back-pressure was released, the aircraft jumped out. 'No one could possibly inadvertently stall a Victor', said 'Hazel'. When he went to Autair to be a Herald captain, Johnny Allam took over as Chief Test Pilot, with Philip 'Spud' Murphy as his deputy.

First production Victor B 1 XA917 took to the air on 1 February 1956. Dressed overall in matt silver, with big black serial numbers, and powered by Sapphire Sa 7 Mk 202 engines rated at 11,000 lbs, XA917 was no sluggard, and on 1 June 1957 it became the largest aircraft in the world to break the sound barrier. On a test flight from Gaydon in Warwickshire, Johnny Allam put XA917 into a shallow dive at 40,000 ft, 'inadvertently' failed to keep an eye on the Machmeter and clocked up 675 mph, which represented Mach 1.02. The double sonic bang was heard from Banbury to Watford.

The Victor was quite stable throughout, giving observer Paul Langston little sensation of what was going on – he landed with the distinction of being the first man to break the sound barrier going backwards. Allam did it to assert the superiority of the Victor over the Vulcan. The Victor did slow rolls, loops and rolls off the top at Farnborough. On 14 October 1958, a Victor broke the UK-Malta speed record by beating the previous best set by a Royal Navy Scimitar fighter by 67 mph.

HP 80 prototype WB771 is seen here in the air in its original silver grey finish in early 1953. The *Sunday Express* described the bomber's crescent wing as 'the greatest step forward in design in modern times.' The hole in the base of the fin provided air for transformer-rectifier cooling and for anti-icing

The second HP 80 prototype, WB775, was photographed at Radlett in March 1955. The aircraft's new red and black colour scheme was chosen by Sir Frederick Handley Page

How did the Victor compare with its arch rival, the Vulcan? The Victor had a greater range and ceiling because of its better maximum lift coefficient and lower drag – Lee calculated that the original Avro 698 wing had about 120 per cent of the transonic drag of the crescent – but low wing loading was the key to the Vulcan's superior manoeuvrability and take-off performance.

The Victor was the more sophisticated design of the pair, especially when it came to systems, but this was not necessarily a good thing. Handley Page's split busbar electrics were way ahead of their time and the Vulcan B 1 had nothing like the same degree of electrical redundancy in the air. But the Victor hydraulics, which involved separate circuits to the different services, operated with a will of their own in the early days. Handley Page men added to their troubles by making the Victor more sophisticated than it need have been.

Minister of Supply Reginald Maudling had no doubt that 'when the Victor gets into the hands of the RAF, it will be the equal in hitting power of any bomber in the world'. The Victor shape remained virtually the same from 1948 right through to production, while Avro had to redesign its Vulcan wing in 1949 when RAE Farnborough proved that bringing the line of maximum thickness sharply forward avoided the loss of effective sweep inboard. Lee already knew this because he had discussed the very topic at Göttingen in 1945. Furthermore, Avro had to put a kink in the Vulcan wing to increase buffet threshold after the first prototype had flown. The fact that Avro was forced to turn its Vulcan into what amounted to a crescent-delta as late as 1955 speaks volumes for the firm foundation on which the Victor was built.

Handley Page notables before their pride and joy. They are, from left to right, W H MacRostie (chief engineer), Chief Test Pilot Sqn Ldr Hedley George 'Hazel' Hazelden', Bob Williams (senior flight observer), Johnny Allam, two unnamed MPs who were about to go for a flight in the aircraft, Reggie Stafford and Sir Frederick Handley Page

TOP OF THE WORLD

Twenty-five production Victor B 1s were ordered in June 1952, with a further 33 (costing £450,000 per basic airframe) following in 1955. Handley Page would have preferred to claw back its research and development costs by continuing the run of B 1s, but 1955 saw the erection of the first Soviet surface-to-air missile (SAM) battery around Moscow, and the RAF was looking towards more potent Victors to keep out of trouble. Studies indicated that a more powerful Victor could reach 56,000 ft over the target while carrying a heavier load further. Twenty-one Victor B 2s were ordered to an as yet unspecified standard on 14 June 1956, to which were added the last eight from the 33 B 1s ordered that were now to be delivered to B 2 standard.

The Victor B 2 was derived from the B 1 by the classic stretching process of fitting more powerful Rolls-Royce Conway engines, more wing area and higher maximum all-up-weight of 223,000 lbs. The B 2 wing area was increased to 2600 sq ft to maintain an adequate manoeuvre margin above the stall at the higher altitudes attainable with more powerful engines. Cedric Vernon, who succeeded Godfrey Lee as Chief Aerodynamicist, supervised the increase in the B 2 wing span from 110 ft to 120 ft. Instead of just tacking five feet onto each tip, which would have pushed the swept wing's centre of gravity too far back, Vernon divided the increase into 18 inches at each wing root and 3 ft 6 in at each tip to keep the aerodynamic centre in the correct relative position.

The specification for the Victor B 2 was issued on 27 February 1958 with a contract for 30 aircraft following on 18 March. The official top speed of the B 2 was Mach 0.92, but Handley Page test pilot Philip 'Spud' Murphy once took a B 2 beyond Mach 0.97. At that speed he found the ailerons locked solid – the only way to recover was to slow down by using the elevators. Although the B 2 had more power that the B 1, it could lock into a super stall as 'Spud' found out the hard way on 23 March 1962.

Flying in XL159 with a mixed Boscombe and Handley Page test crew, the flight trial was to examine low speed handling characteristics following the fitting of production fixed droop leading edges in place of conventional nose flaps as used on

The final shape of the production Victor B 1 in a new matt silver finish. Although the wing area remained the same, overall the B 1 was 4 ft 9 in longer than the prototype and the fin was 15 inches shorter in height. The dorsal fillet was removed from the base of the fin following the loss of WB771 at Cranfield on 14 July 1954, the aircraft's tailplane breaking away during a high-speed calibration run. Only the air intake remained at the very base of the fin

the B 1. During low speed handling – virtually a stall approach – in landing configuration at 16,000 ft, XL159 was mishandled and it entered a stable stall, followed by a flat spin from which the pilots were unable to recover because they found the elevators had no control over attitude.

With the bomber sinking at a rate of about 6000 ft a minute, both pilots ejected safely, the co-pilot at

1000 ft and the captain at 500 ft. Air Electronics Officer (AEO) J Tank abandoned the aircraft successfully, but the other two rear crew members did not make it to the entrance door. XL159 descended almost vertically, crashing onto a farmhouse at Stubton, near Newark-on-Trent, killing two residents and injuring two more. The Victor B 2 had a great element of wing section forward of the engines which led to the super stall, so speed restrictions were imposed. The nose flaps mechanism was also taken out of the leading edge to save weight.

The other main change to the Victor B 2 centred on a new constant-frequency AC electrical system. This sounds very mundane, but in Godfrey Lee's words, 'an unbelievable improvement followed from going over from DC to AC'. The B 2 starboard wing stub now housed a Blackburn-Turbomeca Artouste auxiliary power unit to act as a self-contained source of power and air for engine starting at far-flung dispersals, and to provide airborne emergency power below 25,000 ft.

The B 2's split busbar system was reliable, and even if two alternators failed, the other pair could carry all essential electrical loads. However, if the engines blew out and the main alternators came off line through gross mishandling or from the shock of an exploding nuclear weapon, there was now plenty in reserve. A pair of hydraulic air scoops opened automatically if any two adjacent engines fell below 52 per cent rpm.

These retractable intakes, positioned forward of the fin root, drove two Rotax ram-air turbines which provided enough power above 25,000 ft to keep essential services such as the powered flying controls functioning while the bomber descended to less rarified levels. Once there, the AEO could start the Artouste to take over essential services until the engines were relit and the main alternators brought back on line. From now on, B 2 crews had the satisfaction of knowing that they could rely on the proverbial belt, braces and piece of string – the improved AC system would also meet the additional needs of electronic countermeasures (ECM) and stand-off missiles which were then in the offing.

The first production Victor flies past a Victor car for a Vauxhall publicity photograph

Prototype Victor B 2 XH668, with its increased wingspan and new Rolls-Royce Conway engines, in February 1959

The rationale for V-bomber ECM was defined by the Air Ministry in 1957 as follows;

'All defence systems are dependent on some sort of control and reporting organisation. The basis of this is a ground radar network with a radio link to its fighters in the conventional concept. At a later stage the fighters may be replaced or supplemented by a surface-to-air guided weapons system. This form of defence, however, would still depend on a ground radar system. The ground radar and communications links are vulnerable to jamming, and suggest the most promising method of reducing the effectiveness of the defences and thereby reducing the forecast of the loss-rate of the bomber force.'

An Operational Requirements report prepared in August 1960 on ECM listed the following equipment as being fitted in Victor B 1As and B 2s – one Green Palm voice communications jammer (its creator's name was Palmer), two Blue Diver metric jammers for use against ground radars, three Red Shrimp (named after Mr Shrimpton) S-band jammers 'effective against most ground radars', four Blue Saga passive warning receivers, a Red Steer active rearward-looking tail-warning radar and chaff dispensers 'for sowing gravity-launched Window for the confusion of ground radars'.

You had to stand under the Victor's tail to appreciate the massive size of the ECM power units and transmitter cans which weighed several thousand pounds and were each about the size of a domestic dustbin. All this necessitated a new Victor tail cone which, with six peripheral aerials, resembled an old radial engine with a helmet cowling, while right at the back came the tail warning radar scanner radome.

The second Victor B 2, XH669, appeared at the 1960 Farnborough Airshow still minus its external serial number but now displaying roundels, fin flashes and, most operationally important of all, the extended ECM tail cone. A proposal to convert all B 1s to the B 2 standard was rejected because it would have cost well over half the price of a new B 2 – estimated at £2.5 million in 1962. Consequently, only the newest B 1s were given the ECM tail, and were henceforward known as Victor B 1As.

The B 1A was similar to the B 1 except that the former had a modified cockpit layout and an enhanced ECM capability. The B 1A had a slightly less ambitious ECM fit than the B 2 consisting of a passive radar warning receiver, transmitters under the nose floor, jammers in the rear hatch plus a tail warning radar in a more rounded but slightly shortened tail. All this ECM kit generated lots of heat so a Freon glycol cooling system was fitted in the flash-bomb. On the B 1A the condenser was cooled by ram air from a ventral intake, and it was the blockage of this intake by Window from the front fuselage dispenser that

First generation V-bombers showing their distinctive planforms. Left to right, the delta winged Avro Vulcan, the Vickers Valiant and the crescent-winged Handley Page Victor. The three types would serve alongside each other in the frontline for seven years

The No 232 OCU crew collect the unit's first Victor B 1 (XA931) from Radlett on 28 November 1957. These men are, from left to right, Tony Ringer (Captain), K W Rogers (Co-pilot), P J Evans (Nav Plotter), J E Walton (Nav Radar, although he was called 'bomb aimer' in 1957), and Harry Glendenning (AEO)

Chief Tech Alan Algeo, Gp Capt James Edgar 'Johnnie' Johnson and Flt Lt James Bannister were photographed standing before a Victor B 1 at RAF Cottesmore on 11 September 1958. Chf Tech Algeo is wearing the inverted chevrons of a man in the technical career stream. The 1964 Trade Structure abolished the ranks of senior and master technician. Those of junior and chief technician survived, but their stripes were no longer inverted, their special status simply being indicated by the addition of a four-bladed propeller in the vee of their chevrons (*Ron Case/Keystone/Hulton Archive/Getty Images*)

led to the rear ECM cooling duct on the B 2 being positioned at the base of the fin.

FRONTLINE FLYING

Victors were part of the Medium Bomber Force (MBF), reflecting the aircrafts' range when set against the intercontinental reach of the USAF B-52. Total Research and Development, capital and running costs of the V-force from 1958 to 1962 averaged about £125 million a year, which was not an unreasonable amount to spend on preventing global war, quite apart from fact that the V-force had limited war roles.

The first C-in-C Bomber Command for the V-bomber era was Sir Harry Broadhurst, who grew up on fighters and who had led the Desert Air Force at the age of just 37. His command was divided into two Groups, No 1 Group being responsible for Vulcan bases in Yorkshire and Lincolnshire, and No 3 Group, with its HQ at Mildenhall, which looked after the Victors' and Valiants' Midlands and East Anglian airfields.

Early plans for the MBF envisaged it operating from 12 Class 1 airfields, of which six – Gaydon, Wittering, Wyton, Marham, Honington and Waddington – were virtually complete, and the remaining six (Coningsby, Finningley, Cottesmore, Scampton, Bassingbourn and Watton) were scheduled to be available by the end of 1957. It was originally intended to base operational Victors at Bassingbourn, Watton and Honington, but Bassingbourn and Watton were then dropped off the list to save money, leaving ten Class 1 airfields.

There were ten production Victor B 1s in existence by the time XA927 got airborne on 29 December 1956, but their introduction into frontline service was delayed pending completion of retrospective modifications and the fitment of operational equipment. Victor crew training was undertaken by No 232 Operational Conversion Unit (OCU) at Gaydon, in Warwickshire, which received the 15th production aircraft, XA931, on 28 November 1957. The following day the AOC No 3 Group, AVM Kenneth 'Bing' Cross, flew a one-hour demonstration sortie in the B 1.

Sir Harry Broadhurst gave the first Victor station – Cottesmore, in Rutland – to the top-scoring RAF fighter ace of World War 2 in Europe, Gp Capt J E 'Johnnie' Johnson. Cottesmore was originally designated as a Valiant base, so Johnson went off to do the Valiant conversion, only to be told that the plans had changed and he was to convert to the Victor instead. The first operational Victor unit – No 10 Sqn – received its first B 1, XA935, at Cottesmore on 9 April 1958. No 10 Sqn was established with eight Victors, and on 1 September it was joined by No 15 Sqn at Cottesmore where it subsequently acquired nine aircraft from the 1955 contract. A third unit, No 57 Sqn, was re-formed at Honington, in Suffolk, on 1 January 1959 – it received its first aircraft (XH614) in March and its tenth bomber was to be the last B 1, XH667.

Up goes a B 1 with nose flaps down, looking almost like a flying wing

When XH617 was written off after damage on 19 July 1960, only 24 airframes were upgraded to B 1A standard. Once the last new B 1 had been completed on 31 March 1960, XH613 was flown into Radlett from No 15 Sqn to be re-configured. It completed flight tests in May and was prepared for the final ECM conference on 28 June. By early August the second B 1A, XH618, was also ready to return to Cottesmore. Henceforward, B 1s and B 1As operated side-by-side on No 15 Sqn, as well as at Honington, where No 55 Sqn joined No 57 Sqn on 1 September 1960.

No 10 Sqn remained a wholly B 1 unit throughout its life. Writing to the C-in-C Bomber Command on 10 February 1961 about 'the implications of leaving one of the Victor squadrons without an ECM capability', the Deputy Chief of Air Staff commented that 'we cannot afford all that we are asked to provide', adding 'it costs a million pounds to equip a squadron with ECM'.

In 1962 the first B 1A conversion (XH613) touched the ground with its port wingtip while scrambling at an air display. The captain became a simulator instructor. Shortly afterwards, on 14 June 1962, the same XH613 with a different wingtip was approaching RAF Cottesmore at 1500 ft at the end of the sortie when all four engines ran down after the electrical connectors became disconnected on the throttle box. The Victor was being flown by OC No 15 Sqn, Wg Cdr John Matthews, and on his order to abandon aircraft, the rear crew left the aircraft in less than half a minute. Although one man left the rubber of his flying boots along the fuselage, the entire crew survived.

Some weeks later, a No 10 Sqn aircraft was flying over Bedfordshire when its port wingtip fell off and the crew lost the pressure instruments on the port console. The Victor landed normally, but the wingtip that had fallen off was the same tip that originally belonged to Wg Cdr Matthews' crashed aircraft. There was at least one Cottesmore crew that wished the tip had landed on the Handley Page factory at Radlett!

All eight of No 10 Sqn's Victor B 1s are lined up on the Cottesmore ramp in overcast conditions in the spring of 1958

When Nos 10 and 15 Sqns disbanded in 1964, their place was taken by two B 2 units. No 139 Sqn re-formed at Wittering on 1 February 1962, with XL231 as its first aircraft. A B 2 came off the production line every month and the next unit to receive the aircraft was No 100 Sqn, which re-formed at Wittering on 1 May 1962. These two units were then joined by 'C' Flight of No 232 OCU, which changed its name to the Victor Training Flight on 1 April.

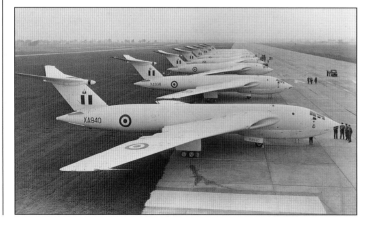

READY FOR WAR

The first operational Victors arrived in service around the time that low-trajectory nuclear-tipped medium range missiles appeared in Soviet satellite territories. These threatened to wreak havoc on the UK within minutes so the 1958 Defence White Paper revealed that measures were being taken to raise the V-force's 'state of readiness, so as to reduce to the minimum the time needed for take-off'. Other action was also being taken 'to increase the security of the bomber force'.

This 'other action' was to disperse the MBF so that all the deterrent eggs were no longer in ten main base baskets. The original plan was to make 57 UK dispersals available to supplement the Class 1 airfields, supported by ten regional weapons storage sites and seven regional servicing airfields. These would then be given the wherewithal to maintain the V-force at instant readiness for 30 days. Although C-in-C Bomber Command said in an unguarded moment that 'we'll use any runway belonging to anyone, provided it's a good one', the '57-Varieties' scheme was so expensive that a compromise was reached whereby 26 dispersal airfields ranging from Lossiemouth in the north of Scotland to St Mawgan in Cornwall and Aldergrove in Northern Ireland supplemented the ten main bases.

Victors began practising dispersals in 1959, and the first Victor 'scramble' within the postulated four-minute warning time of a missile attack was carried out at Cottesmore on 1 April 1959 before Prime Minister Harold Macmillan. Like all new procedures, it took a bit of getting used to – some crew members were still strapping in as they passed 18,000 ft – but regular repeats soon ensured that everyone got the hang of it. Four-aircraft scrambles in 1963 averaged 1 min 54 sec from the order being given to the fourth aircraft lifting off, the best time being 1 min 9 sec and the worst 2 min 47 sec.

As Vulcans and Victors arrived in service, the Valiants were assigned to the Supreme Allied Commander Europe (SACEUR) in 1961 as a Tactical Bomber Force. Several of these aircraft were placed on 15-minute readiness in case of surprise Soviet attack, and on 1 January 1962 this Quick Reaction Alert (QRA) concept was extended to the whole MBF. From now on,

No 15 Sqn Victors perform a formation flypast at their RAF Cottesmore base in the early 1960s

one nuclear armed aircraft from each squadron sat at 15 minutes' readiness by day and by night on the Operational Readiness Platform, 24 hours a day, 365 days a year.

'From a pilot's point of view', declared Handley Page chief test pilot Hazelden, 'the Victor wasn't all that much of a problem. In spite of innovations such as powered controls and nose flaps, it flew like any other aeroplane'. Nevertheless, Bomber Command was very particular about who was allowed to operate the shiny crescent bomber. The average age of Victor pilots in 1957 was about 30. First pilots, who were always captains, had to be rated 'above average', be in possession of at least 1750 first-pilot flying hours,and must have had previous jet as well as four-engined experience, although the latter was considered desirable rather than essential. Co-pilots could get away with 700 first-pilot hours.

Among the rear crew, all of whom had to be recommended by their COs and be 'above average', Nav Plotters had to have completed a Canberra tour, Nav Radars to have passed the radar bombing course at Lindholme and AEOs to have had at least one tour of duty in Bomber, Transport or Coastal Commands. It was an old joke in the early days of the Victor force that you needed 2000 flying hours just to pull the chocks away. After crew conversion on No 232 OCU, which comprised about six weeks ground school plus a similar period of simulator work and some 40-50 flying hours, a Victor crew was ready to join their squadron. New crews were declared Operational once they had proved their worth, and every six months thereafter their bombing and navigation scores were correlated by No 3 Group headquarters. As accuracies improved, a crew would be promoted first to Combat and then to Select status.

It was originally intended that Combat and Select crews would serve together for 5¼ and 7½ years respectively, and to provide further incentive the designation Select Star was added for the *crème de la crème*. Select and Select Star designations were eventually changed to Senior and Command, but either way these classifications were awarded only to crews who were consistently good over a period of years.

Each Victor was entrusted to a specific Crew Chief who went with the aircraft whenever it returned to Handley Page, and who acted as the sixth member of the crew whenever his bomber landed away from base. Yet in spite of this skilled assistance, all aircrew members were required to qualify for servicing certificates so that they could inspect, refuel and turn-round their Victor on their own. The hardest task of all was repacking the tail-brake parachute.

To understand what it was like to fly the Victor, it is worth following a typical No 15 Sqn B 1 training mission in 1960. A Victor crew generally averaged one five-hour training sortie each week, the rest of their time being taken up with ground training, target study or an air test. The crew of five would meet together some three hours before take-off at the Operations Block, which in the V-force replaced the

'Johnnie' Johnson overflies Vandenburg AFB, California, in a B 1 shortly before the first RAF firing of a Thor missile in April 1959. Britain had 60 Thor IRM on loan from the US. In the event of war, they would have blazed a trail for the Victors by wreaking havoc on the Soviet air defence system

squadron crewroom as a self-contained centre for briefing, intelligence and flying clothing.

The first hour would be spent preparing charts, checking weather and diversion airfields, booking bombing ranges, calculating take-off performance and fuel planning. The Nav Radar would also have spent hours previously building up a full radar prediction for the sortie. The mission this day was to consist of two simulated attacks against radar bomb-score units in Newcastle and East Anglia, followed by two long navigation legs up and down the length of the British Isles. After covering some 2500 miles, the Victor and its crew would finish up at Cottesmore where they started.

The next hour would be spent devouring a high protein pre-flight meal and kitting out in flying clothing, followed by collection of in-flight rations and embarkation on a small crew coach with its oxygen supply points for pre-oxygenation. Then it was off across the airfield to the waiting Victor that might be on a dispersed pan several miles away. Once there, the Crew Chief would brief on any minor problems or recent rectification work on the aircraft and the captain would sign for his charge on the Form 700, after which he would walk round the Victor to check some 70 different points externally.

Optimum Victor climb speed was 300 knots. The Sapphires could be left at take-off power for up to ten minutes for maximum rate of climb, but to minimise airframe fatigue the Victor was usually climbed at 250 knots and 98 per cent rpm up to 10,000 ft. Once through the turbulent lower air, speed was increased to 300 knots until it was coincident with the high level climb speed of Mach 0.83. On the B 1A and B 2 a three-position jet pipe temperature control datum could be set to either TAKE-OFF, CLIMB or CRUISE to relieve the pilot of constant throttle adjustment. There were other checks to make as the Victor powered up through the clouds and into the bright blue skies above. Oxygen flow had to be verified at 10,000 ft and cross-checked regularly thereafter, along with cabin pressure. Cabin pressure and temperature controls were only within reach of the co-pilot, and he was soundly berated if he let the cabin get too hot or too cold.

Nineteen-and-a-half minutes after take-off, 160,000 lbs of Victor B 1 would pass through 40,000 ft (it took just under half the time at the same weight in a B 2). On levelling out, the flying pilot would set cruise-climb rpm. As fuel was used and the Victor got lighter, it would

Victor B 1As from No 57 Sqn taxi out at Honington in 1961 to deploy away from their main base

cruise-climb gently up towards 50,000 ft. The first Victors carried Gee, which measured the difference in time required for transmissions from ground stations to reach the bomber in flight. This information was displayed on a cathode ray tube, and from a special Gee grid overprinted on his map, the Nav Plotter would then plot his position to within half-a-mile. But beacon-orientated aids such as Gee could not only be jammed but they were also of too limited range to be of much accurate use on long-range flights to the USSR. Consequently, Victor Plotters were given self-contained navigational devices known as Green Satin and the Ground Position Indicator (GPI).

Green Satin was a radar navigation aid designed for use between 250 ft and 60,000 ft, utilising the Doppler principle to provide continuous indication of the Victor's true groundspeed and drift. Simply stated, when electro-magnetic waves are transmitted from an aircraft towards the ground, some of the waves will be reflected back to be received by the aircraft at a different frequency from that at which they were transmitted. The amount of frequency change is proportional to relative motion between the aircraft and the point of reflection on the ground, and if this point of reflection is on the aircraft's track, then the amount of frequency change can be expressed in terms of groundspeed. This was the basis of the Green Satin system, which transmitted two beams of short burst pulses simultaneously, one looking forward and the other aft of the aircraft, and which could then be measured on return and converted to groundspeed and distance flown.

At the same time the aerials were kept in constant alignment with the aircraft's track so that automatic measurement of the angle between the fore and aft axis of the bomber and the fore and aft axis of the aerials provided drift information. Data from Green Satin was fed into the GPI – an electromechanical computer that was one of the most intricate and wonderful pieces of kit on the Victor, as well as one of the most expensive – which continuously displayed the aircraft's ground position in latitude and longitude on counters.

To cater for the day when some or all of these wonderful aids failed, the crew would practice 'secondary' navigation techniques whereby the Green Satin and GPI were monitored by fixes from the radio compass rather than from the radar. As a further back-stop, the Plotter could always turn his eyes to the heavens, if not for inspiration then at least to 'shoot' the stars by astro-navigation. A periscopic sextant could be fitted into the Victor roof and 'astro' was particularly valuable because it relied only upon the unjammable heavens. At night when practising 'limited' navigational techniques, the Nav Radar would shoot the stars to enable the Plotter to calculate fixes. It was somewhat crude, but a good crew flying precisely and navigating accurately over a featureless sea could coast in after a long 'limited' navex to within an accuracy of 12 miles.

Taking inherent errors into account, the basic accuracy of the Green Satin/GPI combination was two miles along track and 8-12 miles across track in every 1000 miles. To refine this still further the H2S, with its ability to discriminate to within 150 ft, was used to update the navigation equipment. Information from the H2S was fed into the Navigation and Bombing Computer (NBC) Mk 2, built by AEI. Given the age in which it was built, the NBC was an advanced, miniaturised electro-mechanical

XA928 was the 12th production Victor B 1 built, and it is seen here in No 10 Sqn livery. The small black extrusion under the tail was the Victor's 19th tyre – a tail wheel designed to save the fuselage from scraping the runway during a nose-up landing. Later converted into a B 1A, this aircraft served with Nos 57 and 214 Sqns prior to being struck off charge on 16 December 1976

An H2S radar picture of Southend Pier in 1957. The aircraft's position is in the centre of the range circle

device that constantly computed the Victor's track, groundspeed, latitude and longitude.

Although much improved, these avionics were still based on systems used in the Halifax, and they were heavy, rugged, analogue and manpower intensive to maintain and operate. The technology was based on triangle solving, the sole purpose being to generate a plan-range for fixing and weapon aiming calculations. Electrically motored pulleys connected metal tape in the shape of a triangle. The hypotenuse was an analogue of the radar range, obtained from the H2S. The adjacent side was an analogue of barometric height leaving a measure of the opposite side to provide the requisite plan-range. The whole was contained in a heavy metal container similar in size and shape to a dustbin, but the 400-yard system accuracy was quite sufficient for high-level nuclear strike operations.

As such the NBC was the primary fixing aid because, like the eye, the H2S could actually see where it was over the ground. One of the advantages of the H2S Mk 9A over its wartime predecessors lay in its electronic markers. On the quarter-million bombing scale these markers consisted of a variable range circle and bearing marker whose intersection always defined the electronic centre of the radar screen, and they acted as a very accurate bomb-sight graticule.

To have some objective means of assessing accuracy, crews usually operated against Radar Bomb Score Units (RBSUs). These moved around for the sake of variety, but the procedures were always the same. The AEO would call up the RBSU with details of the scheduled attack – for example a road crossing a stream in hilly country. The Nav Radar switched on a radio tone signal as he approached release point, and when the tone cut off, the RBSU marked the point where the crew would have released their bomb. The RBSU controllers went into their ballistics tables to work out the forward throw – ballistic bombs had a forward throw of around eight miles – and plot the theoretical point of impact. The bombing score was then passed back to the aircraft as a Delta Hotel (Direct Hit) or error in terms of bearing and distance in yards – over a six-month

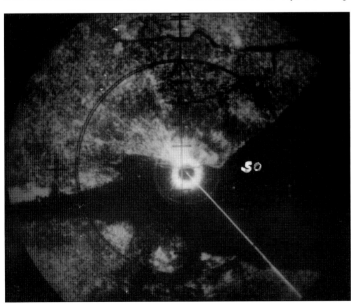

A Chief Tech talks to the aircrew via the external intercom during their start-up checks. It was cold and bleak on the average V-bomber pan

classification period, a Combat crew was expected to achieve bombing accuracies to within 650 yards, a Select crew to within 400 yards and a Select Star crew to within 350 yards.

AVM 'Bing' Cross at HQ No 3 Group firmly believed that 'what matters is what you could do and how you show it before you do it'. States of readiness in 1961 ranged from 'Blue Alert', or 30 minutes warning, to the cockpit readiness of 'Amber Alert'. No-notice exercise dispersals of the whole MBF were known as *Micky Finns*. *Mayflights* were exercises in which, on receipt of the relevant alert, certain aircraft and crews from a particular squadron were detached as rapidly as possible to the dispersal airfield.

When on dispersal, No 10 Sqn Victors undertook a pre-planned *Kinsman* in June 1960, the purpose being to practise day-to-day operating from Boscombe Down. Early *Mayflights* usually ended with a *Matador* exercise to test the UK air defences. *Lone Ranger* and *Western Ranger* flights by single aircraft were common, the former eastwards to Wildenrath, Luqa, El Adem, Nairobi, Salisbury or the Persian Gulf and the latter westwards, chiefly to Offutt AFB, Nebraska.

Eventually concrete aircraft hardstandings known as Operational Readiness Platforms (ORPs) were laid adjacent to most runway thresholds, purpose-built crew caravans resembling railway sleeping cars being positioned close by and temporary command posts established with efficient lines of communication. Individual starting of the Victor B 1's Sapphire engines was too time-consuming, so Sqn Ldr J C Dixon designed the 'Simstart' trolley which, with its great array of batteries, enabled a Crew Chief to start all four engines in rapid succession while his aircrew were strapping in. The Victor B 2 retrofit programme subsequently incorporated an internal rapid start facility whereby the captain pressed one button and fuel/air combustors would fire up all four Conways in 15 seconds. All the Victor crews then had to do was roll forward off the ORP and roar into the sky in quick succession.

OPERATIONAL EFFECTIVENESS

On 16 July 1958, Prime Minister Harold Macmillan reaffirmed the purpose of the British independent nuclear capability as;

'(a) To retain our special relation with the United States and, through it, our influence in world affairs, and, especially, our right to have a voice in the final issue of peace or war.

'(b) To make a definite, though limited, contribution to the total nuclear strength of the West – while recognising that the United States must continue to play the major part in maintaining the balance of nuclear power.

'(c) To enable us, by threatening to use our independent nuclear power, to secure the United States' cooperation in a situation in which their interests were less immediately threatened than our own.

'(d) To make sure that, in a nuclear war, sufficient attention is given to certain Soviet targets which are of greater importance to us than to the United States (particularly bomber airfields and missile-launching sites from which attacks on the UK could be mounted).

'To constitute a minimum deterrent and serve the purposes for which it is intended, the V-force must be operationally viable – i.e. it must be sufficiently large and well equipped to deliver enough bombs to inflict an adequate measure of destruction in Russia.'

Talks in early 1957 between the RAF Chief of Air Staff and his USAF opposite number resulted in the targeting plans of US Strategic Air Command (SAC) and RAF Bomber Command being closely dovetailed. Consequently, Bomber Command had the advantage of knowing that its progress in a war would be facilitated by American missiles, but it was not just a one-sided arrangement. 'Some of our targets', recalled one AEO, 'looked as if they were clearing the way for someone else', and in the words of former Deputy Chief of Air Staff, AM Sir Geoffrey Tuttle, 'we taught the Americans a hell of a lot. We had to face many of the problems first – we were nearer to the USSR, we were threatened long before the Americans were, and therefore we had the incentive to survive much sooner than they did'.

Under the Single Integrated Operational Plan (SIOP), total US/RAF strategic air forces were deemed sufficient to cover all Soviet targets, including airfields and air defence. Bomber Command's contribution was given as 92 aircraft in October 1958, increasing to 108 by June 1959. Some 106 targets were allocated to Bomber Command as follows – 69 cities, which were centres of government or of other military significance, 17 long-range air force airfields that were part of the Soviet nuclear threat and 20 elements of the Soviet *PVO-Strany* air defence system

If the Cold War had turned hot, how would the Victors have gone about their business? Eventually, the international situation would have become so strained that HQ Bomber Command at High Wycombe would have been told to disperse the V-force. There, the individual groups of aircraft would have stayed at increasing states of readiness. Each aeroplane was connected to reality by an umbilical tele-scramble link to the Bomber Controller at High Wycombe, and on the command from the War Room in London he would have been instructed by his C-in-C to order the V-force to start engines and then to 'Scramble'. On airfields from the very north of Scotland to Cornwall, up to 16 engines would have started simultaneously.

A tall 'giraffe' platform was necessary to service the rudder power flying units in the high tail. B 1 XA931 was assigned to No 232 OCU when this photograph was taken. Aside from a brief spell with No 10 Sqn, this aircraft remained with the OCU throughout its service life, which ended when it was struck off charge on 30 April 1974

Throttles would be opened and bombers would take off in quick succession until, long before four minutes had passed, there would be nothing left to show where they had been save some turbulent and darkened air and the pungent smell of burnt aviation fuel.

Radio silence would be maintained to prevent detection. The systems were so duplicated as to carry on regardless, and all the years of toil and training with simulated equipment failures had been endured in preparation for just this moment. There would have been nowhere else to go but forward so long as the wings remained attached and at least two engines were working.

The great advantage of the manned bomber over the missile is that the former could be launched to make a potential aggressor withdraw from the brink, whereas there is no way of bringing back a missile. V-bombers would have met timing points and specific positions in order to comply with the coordinated raid plan. The routes were planned to fly out to a 100-mile arc based on Flamborough Head, then tracks would fly to a straight line position known as the 'Go/No Go' line. No Victors were allowed to cross this line without the crew receiving a valid coded message. If no message came, there was no assuming that Whitehall had been obliterated – the V-force had to turn back. On the other hand, once the 'Go' message had been received there was no mechanism for 'recalling the dogs after they had been unleashed'.

Victors would have flown dense parallel tracks toward a few chosen penetrations points, each around four to five miles wide, in as short a period as possible. The MBF would have entered the Soviet Union in loose cells of six anywhere at speeds up to Mach 0.93. Victor B 2s would have gently "cruise climbed" upwards as fuel was used and weight reduced to be above 50,000 ft.

The higher an aircraft goes, the earlier the ground radar can detect it, so carefully pre-planned routes were essential. As Soviet radars could detect a Victor 200 miles away, some would have flown a longer and more circuitous route than might otherwise have been necessary. Eventually, though, the bombers would have to run the gauntlet of the opposing air defences. Intelligence sources tried to predict the points where the defences might be weakest but those targets worth attacking would also be those that were best protected, and this was where ECM came in.

Victor ECM consisted of a three-fold system to jam both active and passive radar systems, as well as disrupting the enemy communications radio. It was designed to be effective against radar-guided missiles as well as ground radar systems, thereby seriously embarrassing the defenders. The Victor's impressive ECM suite provided a reasonable degree of situational awareness, and the crew aimed to avoid or evade the ground or air defences by jamming their control and warning radars with noise. Noise jamming was a 'brute force' expedient in that it relied on 'out-shouting' rather than deceiving the opposition. The Soviets could point their fighters straight at the high flier if they got good radar control from the ground to put them there, but if they had not got it, the interception of a 50,000 ft Mach 0.93 Victor became a bit of a lottery.

The AEO, who was responsible for the Victor's electrical system and handled a great deal of communications (particularly long-range HF radio traffic), looked after the jammers. In the AEO's 'office', the

EW controls were in front of him on the bulkhead, with a schematic of the electrical system and its various controls to his right on the port side wall of the cabin.

The three Red Shrimps, each of which operated in two modulation modes between 2.5 and 3 GHz, were intended to jam the gun-laying radars controlling 57 mm and 76 mm AAA and the 'Low Blow' radar acquisition element of the SA-3 missile. The Blue Divers, which had notched aerials at the wingtips, operated in the metric frequency range and were intended to jam Soviet early warning radars. They radiated plenty of power, and it was said that during an air defence exercise, just as the nation was settling down to watch the soap opera of the day, a group of V-bombers switched on their Blue Divers and wiped out all the television signals!

One Victor AEO recalls flying EW runs against the calibration facility operated by No 81 Signals Unit at Benbecula, on Stornaway, with timed sequential switching of the gear to check it was functioning. 'It was the L Band jammer that could get you into trouble. If I remember rightly it came towards the end of the run, the switch was not on the EW panel, and if you forgot to switch it off, it would take out Scottish TV as you flew south – usually for a bollocking after landing back at Wittering'.

The impressive jamming capability of the Victor B 2 was optimised for high-level attack against the USSR in the late 1950s and early 1960s. In a coordinated attack over a relatively broad front with close to 100 V-bombers jamming on full power to provide mutually reinforcing protection, the Divers would have denied the Soviets early warning and the Shrimps would have negated their anti-aircraft missiles and guns. Soviet fighter aircraft of the time used only four VHF channels for their radio communications, and the Victor's Green Palm, with its antenna at the top of the fin (which emitted a deafening noise like a cross between a continental police siren and the bagpipes), was tuned to jam those four frequencies. There was a good chance therefore that the AEO might be able to prevent a Soviet fighter from ever receiving enough instructions to attain radar or visual contact.

Victor B 1As and B 2s were also provided with a Blue Saga radar warning receiver – a first generation passive warning receiver which relied on four sets of small stub antennas mounted 'quadrangularly' on the uppersurface of the nose and the lower tail. Blue Saga received signals in the bands roughly 2.5 to 12 GHz. Its display comprised two orange lights, one for S-Band and one for C/X-Bands, which illuminated when a signal reached a pre-determined PRF (pulse-repetition frequency) threshold or pulse width. The AEO would monitor the PRF audio tone in his headset and switch between the four sets of antennae to determine the quadrant from which the signal was being received. This was a pretty 'mandraulic' device and it was slow by modern standards but, with practice, the AEOs became quite adept at detecting, identifying and taking action against incoming threat signals.

The V-bomber H2S radar had a modification called Fishpool which under certain circumstances could detect fighters around and below, so the Nav Radar could sometimes see the fighter climbing. He would pass this information to the crew and the AEO could take over the running commentary as the fighter swept in behind and into the ken of his

25

backward-looking tail warning radar. This evolved from the Green Willow Airborne Intercept (AI) radar developed as a backup for the English Electric Lightning. A team at Telecommunications Research Establishment Malvern recognised that, with a minimum of re-design, Green Willow could be adapted to meet a requirement issued in 1956 for V-bomber tail warning radar. During trials in 1958, the radar (christened Red Steer after Jerry Steer, a Malvern liaison officer) demonstrated a 75 per cent certainty of detecting a Hawker Hunter making a 'straight tail on' approach at ten nautical miles, rising to 100 per cent certainty of detection at eight nautical miles.

Even if an interceptor pilot got into a tail position, bundles of chaff or 'Window' – tinfoil strips which produced echoes equal in magnitude to those of an aircraft – might confuse him if he was relying on his airborne radar. The Victor carried thousands of bundles of rapid-blooming chaff, pre-cut to various lengths so as to give wideband frequency coverage. They were stored within the wing, just aft of the main undercarriage legs, in what were inevitably known as 'window boxes', two per side. Chaff was dispensed through apertures in the underside of the wing which looked like letter-boxes. Later on the crews were provided with 192 Magnesium Teflon Viton compound flares which allegedly had a sufficient IR signature to seduce a missile away from Victor jet pipes. A substantial metal pin about two inches long was ejected whenever the flares were fired, so in peacetime AEOs could only dispense them over the sea, and then only after ensuring that they were not going to sink any ships. Nevertheless, they did light up the sky and were quite spectacular!

The main Soviet radar-guided air-to-air missile of the time had to be launched when its fighter's wings were virtually level, otherwise the missile fell out of the directing beam. 'One must not exaggerate the advantages of these new (rocket) weapons', wrote Soviet missile expert Gen Pokrovsky. 'The more automatic any procedure becomes, the easier it becomes for the enemy to jam that procedure. Manoeuvre can easily fool such automatic weapons'. However, a Victor turning to avoid a fighter was being prevented from flying towards its target.

Victor ECM was largely an extension of World War 2 barrage jamming, albeit with much greater intensity. There was little sophistication involved – the Victor ECM equipment did not respond with specific reactions to counter individual threats in the way that modern systems do. V-force crews relied on brute force, and lots of it. Jammers were simply switched on at a particular point on the outbound track and left to radiate on a pre-set range of frequencies, regardless of whether or not there was an actual threat to be countered.

'I don't recall any EW 'tactics' as such', said one Victor B 2 AEO, 'and when we switched on all of the EW gear at the designated time, we

This view of the Red Steer tail warning radar illustrates the size of the ECM gear that Handley Page had to fit into later Victors

all assumed that our aircraft would be covered in an invisible "Star Wars type" shield'. It might have been rather crude, but through all the white noise the Victors would try to sneak past undetected. And they would have gone in behind the Thors and other ballistic missiles, which if they did not hit air defence centres would certainly have played havoc with telephone lines and fragile aerial arrays when they exploded.

Despite all the prophets of doom, the anti-aircraft missile did not make the bomber obsolete overnight. A Joint Intelligence Committee report forecast that Soviet city defences would be complete by 1961. Based on this assessment, Bomber Command aimed to reduce the effectiveness of SAM defences by the use of ECM, tactical routeing to avoid known missile sites and increasing the number of V-bombers allocated to the more important and heavily defended targets.

Victor crews knew where most of the SA-2 SAM sites were located and they could hear the SAM radars looking for them, so consequently they could detour around them. However, by 1962 there were too many SA-2 sites in existence to avoid them all, so the AEO would try to barrage jam the missile radar and feed it false chaff targets while the pilot weaved around track to prevent the missile-control computers from ever having enough steady and reliable information on which to base a launch.

Straight and level attacks from as high as possible were Type 2 attacks. Once Gary Powers' U-2 was shot down by an SA-2 SAM at 70,000 ft on 1 May 1960, the V-force changed to a Type 2A high-level evasive bombing run. Some 40 miles from the target, the bomber would pull 1.5g through 45 degrees. Wings would be levelled for 15 seconds, before a 90-degree turn in the opposite direction. Wings would be levelled again for 30 seconds before the manoeuvre was repeated. The next steady leg was 15 seconds before the aircraft was rolled onto its attack heading about 15 miles from the target. The SA-2 SAM system needed 60 seconds of uninterrupted lock-on to make good, and all the Type 2A jinking was designed to thwart that objective.

The trained men at the SA-2 site would have been more difficult to fool than a machine, and the barrage of three missiles they fired would have increased their chances of overcoming jamming, but an SA-2 system needed a good 60 seconds from initial acquisition to the end of the engagement, and continuously effective jamming for any 15-second period within that time would probably be enough to avoid destruction. In addition, despite the demarcation between missile and fighter zones, some Soviet fighters would have hung onto their bombers as the latter entered the SAM radar cover, and this would have complicated the issue for missile controllers on the ground.

Nevertheless, the SAMs too would have taken their toll of the intruders, especially as the groups of aircraft would by now have split up to go towards their respective targets. Once through the coastal SAM screen and out into the hinterland, the V-force would disperse, although some notional corridors were used. Aircraft would join the corridor at some point while others would leave. It was designed to suggest that two bombers were flying in a particular direction towards a particular target.

Having worked his way into the USSR, a Nav Radar could often see his aiming point from 160 miles away, and the usual procedure was to home to an easily identifiable Initial Point some 60 miles from weapon relcasc, where the navigation and bombing computers could be finally updated accurately. At 40 miles to weapon release, the Nav Radar would change over to his larger bombing scale and place the target under his aiming markers by means of his 'joystick'. If the target response was weak or impossible to identify, the bombing run could still be pressed home provided there was an identifiable reference point close by. The coordinate distances of the target from the reference point could be set on 'offset' dials and the aircraft automatically homed to the correct release point.

Outside, the fighters might have been temporarily shaken off, but the warning receivers would have been chattering frantically as they picked up a crescendo of radar signals. The windscreen blinds would have been down, but even so the occasional flash of light might have crept in underneath from an exploding bomb or missile. Once the target or 'offsets' were in, the computers could do the rest down to feeding steering information directly into the autopilot. The Navigation and Bombing System was a marvellous piece of equipment which even opened the bomb doors automatically just before the point where it computed that the bomb should be dropped. The weapon could be released automatically or manually, and as the white flag dropped on the Military Flight System indicator showing that the weapon had left the bomb-bay, the pilot would rack his Victor round into the escape manoeuvre to avoid overflying the detonation, close the bomb-bay doors and beat a retreat.

Crews were given return routes, and although the problems of coordinating the returning aircraft back through outbound waves of SAC bombers and into Western airspace without being shot down were not insuperable, no one postulated how many of them would get back, and there was never any intention of sending the remnants back over the USSR on the morrow. The best hope for survival probably lay in closing down two engines to conserve whatever fuel was still lapping the bottom of the tanks and heading for the British Mediterranean bases to the south.

If it had come to the worst, the Victors could have ranged at high level as far east as Magnitogorsk, on the Ural River. Within this compass lay the strategically vital Volga oilfield, the Ukrainian iron and steel-making region and three-quarters of the 72 cities of the USSR that the 1959 census identified as having populations in excess of 200,000.

Looking back, 'Johnnie' Johnson thought that his aircraft would have been very vulnerable if they had gone in during daylight independently from the US. But Johnson, whose firsthand experience of bomber and fighter operations was second to none, believed that as many as 85-90 per cent of the V-force would have got through at night as part of a coordinated US-UK operation. He would have backed his ECM-equipped Victors with their highly skilled crews against the Soviet air defences of the time, and his boss at HQ Bomber Command, Sir Harry Broadhurst, was equally convinced that his force was good enough to deter a potential enemy from committing the supreme act of folly.

When the Fylingdales Ballistic Missile Warning Radar came on line, and one Victor and crew from each squadron sat on permanent QRA on main base ORPs to guard against a surprise attack, the Victor force was finally in a position to live up to Bomber Command's motto of 'Strike Hard, Strike Sure' – and on the instant.

BLUE STEEL AND SKYBOLT

Blue Danube was the first in a family of colourfully named and wholly British-made nuclear weapons that became more compact and more powerful over the years. Blue Danube was a kiloton-range weapon, but after the US and USSR tested thermonuclear devices, the UK government decided on 16 June 1954 to authorise hydrogen bomb production. Although Victor WB775 completed bombing trials with a simulated Blue Danube in April 1956, Victor B 1s and B 1As carried Blue Danube only until Yellow Sun megaton weapons entered service. Victor B 1/1As carried Yellow Sun from 1960, with Yellow Sun 1 having a 0.5 megaton warhead and Yellow Sun 2 double that.

Both Yellow Suns were 3000 lb lighter than the 10,000-lb Blue Danube, but they were all 'free-fall' weapons which meant that their Victor carriers had to approach to within a few miles of the targets that were increasingly going to be protected by SAM defences. 'We've got to get away from this free-falling bomb business as quickly as possible', wrote C-in-C Bomber Command in 1952, and a Handley Page proposal for a faster and higher flying Phase 4 Victor was turned down by the Air Staff early in 1957 because although the bomber promised to be capable of transonic flight, it was unable to carry a stand-off missile.

Operational Requirement (OR) 1132 – 'A Propelled Air-to-Surface Missile for the V-class Bombers' to become known as Blue Steel – was issued on 3 September 1954. The OR Branch view was that this inertially-guided missile 'should result in an extension of the useful life of the V-bomber force and should also enable more accurate bombing of targets by the utilisation of the best radar offset aiming point within the range of 100 nautical miles'. Referred to by the Treasury as 'a powered megaton bomb', Blue Steel was expected to be available by 1960 'to maintain the capacity of the V-force to attack deep-penetration targets in spite of the expected development of the Russian SAM defences'.

Victor B 1 XA930, weighing 190,000 lbs, roars off from Hatfield with a de Havilland Spectre rocket pack below each engine bay – the only time such a take-off fit was trialled. Designed to assist take-offs from short, dispersed airfields, each Spectre pushed out around 8000 lbs of thrust, and was to be jettisoned after launch. When it became clear that Victors B 2s, with their much more powerful Conway engines, did not need such enhancements, the Spectre programme was cancelled on 23 July 1959. When its time as a trials aircraft was over, XA930 was initially upgraded into a B 1A. Some years later it was converted into a Victor K 1 tanker. Having served with Nos 10, 55 (twice), 57 and 214 Sqns, and No 232 OCU, XA930 was struck off charge on 17 April 1975

Designed as a rocket vehicle to fly at Mach 3, Blue Steel had a stainless steel structure to withstand kinetic heating, delta-shaped flying surfaces and a pure inertial navigation system that required no radio communications after launch for course correction over its 150 statute mile range. A special high test peroxide(storable)/kerosene rocket motor named the Stentor was designed and built by Armstrong Siddeley of Coventry to power the weapon. Marconi Elliot of Rochester provided the inertia navigator, whose feedback accelerometers had the phenomenal accuracy of one in a billion. There was no US input into the design.

Neither the Vulcan nor the Victor had been designed to take a stand-off weapon like Blue Steel. On-board systems were different on both, which was unhelpful, especially when it was realised that refrigeration for both warhead and navigation systems would be needed when mated to the aircraft and in missile flight. It was difficult to find extra space in the cockpit for the missile monitoring and system controls especially during flight trials, when even more radio telemetry and instruments were required. It would have been preferable to re-design the Victor cockpit controls after the trials phase to make them more ergonomically efficient, but with delays caused by manufacturing difficulties and production line pressures, there was insufficient time.

Avro's Weapons Research Division at Woodford was awarded a development contract for the Blue Steel stand-off bomb to be mounted with the Vulcan and Victor B 2. The in-service version of Blue Steel was working by 1960. After being shown at the 1961 Farnborough Show with Blue Steel underneath, XL161 went from Radlett to Woodford to begin compatibility trials with the missile in December 1961. Three B 2s (XH674, XH675 and XL161) were allocated to Blue Steel development trials at Woodford and Edinburgh Field, Adelaide, some 250 miles south of the Woomera range. Two million data points were retrieved from each flight, which were then returned to the UK for interpretation.

Victors were given official clearance to carry Blue Steel, including release of the missile up to Mach 0.84 and 55,000 ft, thereby allowing XL161 to carry out live firings over Australia. During one of these on 17 August 1962, XL161 was being flown by a civilian test crew in the climb to 50,000 ft when a leak in the second pilot's pitot static system around 47,000 ft caused the auto Mach trimmer to run fully out and apply a rearward force to the control column. The co-pilot's Machmeter read Mach 1.03 (way above the permissible limit), but the first pilot's

XH668, the first production B 2, at Radlett on 13 March 1959. It still retained the B 1 fin root, and the ram air turbines are extended forward of the fin. XH668 was also distinguished by the big bulges in place of the nose 'nostrils'. These were an attempt to reduce loud noises in the ducting, but this problem was eventually cured by stiffening up the pipes and fitting small vortex generators around the nostril intakes. XH668 was lost during flight trials over St Brides' Bay, off the Pembrokeshire coast, on 20 August 1959 when a pitot head vibrated loose

XH669 was photographed in flight on 8 April 1960. Unlike XH668, it has the nostrils restored and a new fin root to house the intakes providing ram air for cooling the rear ECM gear and for anti-icing. Initially serving with the Wittering Wing, XH669 was eventually converted into a K 2 and flown by Nos 55 and 57 Sqns. The aircraft suffered a fire in flight on 21 June 1990, and although the crew landed it safely, XH669 was not repaired. The K 2 was eventually used for fire practice at RAF Waddington

Machmeter correctly indicated Mach 0.76. Thinking that he had excessive speed, the first pilot reacted to the second pilot's instrument by throttling back and extending the air brakes, thus reducing speed. The aircraft stalled and pitched up, the pilot lost control and the aircraft spun. Recovery was not achieved until the captain thought to stream the landing brake parachute and use it as an anti-spin device. That really was coping under pressure and XL161 returned to level flight at 17,000 ft.

Having completed B 2 production and B 1A retrofits by early 1963, Handley Page was then free to modify Victor B 2s to carry the stand-off missile. 'The Victor was an awful aeroplane to get Blue Steel on because of its limited ground clearance', said one Avro Weapons Division man, but Handley Page solved the problem if only to thwart Avro, which some believed had deliberately set out to build a missile that would be too large to fit under anything except the Vulcan. In the end, Blue Steel ground clearance under an already low-slung Victor was a mere 14 inches. The upper Blue Steel fin had to be removed to install it and the lower fin was folded prior to take-off. Its carriage demanded no special take-off rotation or landing flare-out technique, just extra care.

Aircraft modified to carry Blue Steel had their existing bomb doors removed and replaced by fairings secured to the fuselage by quick release fasteners. These fairings fitted snugly around the missile with a rubber seal strip in between. Cutaway secondary bomb doors were then fitted, which closed after the missile had been fired. Thereafter the underside reverted to the normal contours of a conventional Victor bomber.

Inside the bomb-bay was the Blue Steel carrier, which consisted of a waisted box structure secured by strong points to the roof. The missile was held in place by four crutches mounted at the corners of the carrier, each crutch having a contoured face that was maintained in the correct position relative to the missile by a guide rod. All the main services to the missile (hot air, coolant and arming electrics) passed through the carrier beam. The hydraulic jack attached to the hoist beam in the bomb-bay

Inching Blue Steel under XL158. Because of limited ground clearance, the weapon's top fin was only fitted once it was mounted to the Victor. The missile was elevated by hand-pumped hydraulics to meet the carrier beam in the bomb-bay, and connecting missile to aircraft took five men 30 minutes. The underwing divided scoop above the missile was the Artouste APU duct

XL158, sporting a No 139 Sqn crest at RAF Wittering, shows its new ECM-tail with Red Steer tail warning radar dome at the very back. The aircrew member is wearing a partial pressure jerkin designed to protect him in the event of cockpit pressurisation failure above 50,000 ft

roof was secured to a Pneumatic Release Unit that sent the missile on its way. Blue Steel control panels were fitted inside the cockpit, mainly at the rear crew position, but the flight safety lock switches were mounted alongside the captain.

The performance penalty with Blue Steel slung underneath was officially given as two per cent, yet it is interesting to note that the 1961 Boscombe trials to clear satisfactory release of Blue Steel from a B 2 had to be conducted at 51,000 ft because the chase aeroplane – one of the latest Javelin all-weather fighters – could not climb any higher! Initially, a Blue Steel Victor could be converted back to the free-fall role within 30 hours, but as more and more missile modifications and avionics changes were incorporated, this dualism became less and less realistic over the years.

The B 2 retrofit programme did more than just fit Blue Steel. Early Victor B 2s had been powered by Conway Co 11 engines rated at 17,250 lbs thrust, but in 1961 XL159 was sent back to Handley Page for installation of uprated Co 17s capable of 20,600 lbs thrust each. Power surging occurred even though the bypass ratio of the new engine was reduced to match the Victor's limited rib spacing. Indeed, it was this structural limitation that prevented the Victor from ever realising the full potential of the Co 22, which was pod-mounted on the VC10 airliner.

Fixed droop leading edges with vortex-generating 'turbulators' were incorporated during manufacture on the last production B 2s (XM714-XM718), but the remainder were modified during the retrofit programme. The opportunity was also taken to modify and extend the ECM fit following trials in April 1962 when XH671 tested the equipment for compatibility with Blue Steel. Finally, nacelle-like fairings were attached to the upper surfaces of the B 2 wing. Designated 'Küchemann carrots' or 'Whitcomb bodies', depending on whether you credited their design to Dr Dietrich Küchemann of RAE Farnborough or Dr Richard Whitcomb of the Langley Laboratory in America, these fairings 'area-ruled' the wing and acted as fences to improve performance by weakening the shock waves, thereby delaying separation of the boundary layer.

The combination of Conway Co 17 engines and Whitcomb bodies

conferred better performance at height with minimal weight change. Having installed the fairings, Handley Page then found that they could provide stowage for the Window dispensers that had to be removed from under the centreline because Blue Steel resented tin-foil strips going into its controls and orifices.

XL164 was the trials aircraft for what was known as the Victor B 2R (Retrofit) standard. XL511 was the first B 2R to be delivered to Wittering in July 1963, followed by XL512 and XL513, enabling No 139 Sqn to fly its first sortie with a training missile on 24 October. On average it took 15 hours to train a Victor crew in the use of Blue Steel, and No 139 Sqn become operational with the missile before the end of the year. B 2R aircraft were finished in high-reflectivity gloss white paint with pale blue and pink national markings and pale blue serial numbers.

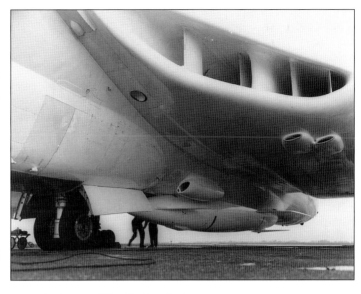

A snug fit. The bottom Blue Steel fin is folded to clear the ground. The aircraft captain had a fin fold switch on his left hand side in the cockpit

As it equipped with B 2Rs, No 139 Sqn passed its free-fall B 2s back to the retrofit line or to No 100 Sqn. The latter received its first B 2R, XL160, on 16 January 1964, followed by XH675 on 17 February and then XM717. There was an element of musical chairs as aircraft moved back and forth between Wittering units and Radlett, and the plan was also affected by the unfortunate crash of XM714 just after it took off from Wittering on 20 March 1963. The blazing wreck missed the tiny village of Barnack by 80 yards, but five of the six men on board died – only the co-pilot, Flt Lt Benny Jackson, managed to eject and survive. XM714 was replaced by the last Victor of all, XM718, on 2 May, but it was to be a short substitution because the aircraft made a heavy landing at Wittering in October and had to be returned to Radlett for repair.

Back in 1962, C-in-C Bomber Command had complained that Handley Page had 'fallen down badly in the production of the Victor Mk 2 Blue Steel'. Originally there were to have been six Blue Steel squadrons, three of Vulcans and three of Victors, but the delay in getting the Victor B 2Rs into service led to an Air Council decision on 10 February 1964 to allot

XH675 with Blue Steel fin folded down. Another WIttering Wing aircraft, XH675 was also converted into a K 2 and served with Nos 57 and 55 Sqns. The veteran machine was finally struck off charge in June 1991

the third Victor B 2 squadron to the strategic reconnaissance role. In all, 21 Victor B 2s were converted into B 2Rs. Wittering's two B 2 units used Gaydon, Wyton and Coltishall as near dispersals and St Mawgan as their distant one.

The production contract placed on 15 December 1960 was for 75 stand-off missiles, but this total was subsequently reduced to 57 Mk 1 Blue Steels, which were all that entered RAF service. The Blue Steel inertial navigation system was integrated with the navigation equipment of the parent Victor, and the former was so accurate that the missile navigated the aircraft on the outbound leg while the Nav Radar periodically fed in H2S fixes to realign the system.

The inertial navigator suffered from a gyro wander rate of up to one degree per hour, so as near to the release point as possible the Nav Radar took a final Release Point Fix to update the missile flight rules computer with the exact aircraft position, the direction in which it was heading, airspeed, altitude, acceleration and attitude date, as well as the relative position of the target. The captain operated a switch to unfold the bottom stabilising fin, and the missile was released from 50,000 ft. For four seconds it fell freely for about 300 ft to clear the aircraft, and then the Stentor liquid-fuelled rocket motor fired. Two seconds later the missile controls unlocked and it accelerated up to its pre-set height.

The Stentor was a relatively inexpensive engine, and its main combustion chamber produced 16,000 lbs of thrust. This was supplemented by a secondary

A B 2 lands and streams at a very damp Farnborough in the early 1960s. When the brake chute was streamed in a strong crosswind, the resulting yaw could be violent, and quick action was needed on the rudders and nosewheel steering to counteract the swing

Blue Steel-toting B 2R XL158 of No 139 Sqn performs a low-level flypast in its new gloss white finish with pale blue and pink markings and pale blue serial numbers. Becoming a part of the pooled Wittering Wing in the early 1960s, the bomber was subsequently flown by the Victor Training Flight at RAF Wyton. Converted into a K 2, XL158 served with Nos 55 (twice) and 57 Sqns, before becoming one of the last Victors retired from RAF service in October 1993

Left
A dummy Yellow Sun 2 – the most powerful British H-bomb – being loaded into a Victor bomb-bay. Training rounds were painted blue, while the real thing was painted white (*RAF Air Historical Branch*)

This official briefing slide was used to explain the Blue Steel method of high level delivery

chamber that added an extra 4000 lbs of thrust, and the pair together were capable of sending the missile up vertically to 110,000 ft. However, such a profile was not conducive to range, so the main combustion chamber drove the missile up to 70,000 ft, where it levelled off. The main chamber then cut out and the secondary took over, this being enough in the rarefied air to sustain the missile at a speed of Mach 2.5.

In this fashion Blue Steel hurtled along under the control of its flight rules computer, which calculated every change of velocity and direction from ultra-sensitive acceleration measurements made from within the missile. In simple terms the weapon knew its distance out and its distance off from the target, and it tried to fly the most direct route in between. Directional control was on the 'twist and steer' principle by which each turn was begun by rolling with the inboard ailerons on the rear mounted delta wing, and then maintained by increasing lift on the small delta-shaped foreplanes. The inertial navigator was forever looking for a particular dive angle to the target, and when it got there after approximately four minutes on a 100-mile flight, down the missile went at between Mach 1.5 and Mach 1.8 to penetrate the defences. Blue Steel carried the Red Snow megaton warhead used in Yellow Sun 2.

Blue Steel was an excellent stand-off weapon in that it required no signals from outside to go about its business, it could not be jammed or diverted by countermeasures and its profile could be infinitely varied from short distances at very high speed to 200 miles range with a descent speed of Mach 0.8-0.9. On trials in Australia using a distinctive well in the desert as an aiming point, the missile regularly landed within 100 yards. It was estimated that a Blue Steel released over London could have put a megaton of H-bomb onto Manchester to within 700 yards. 'Out of the last ten shots at Woomera', said C-in-C Bomber Command in 1963, 'nine have been completely successful. The Blue Steel can stand comparison with any other missile system being developed anywhere in the world'.

In August 1957, the UK Defence Committee approved a V-force frontline strength of 144 aircraft, including 104 Victor B 2s, which justified the final order for 30 examples on 18 March 1958. Thereafter, the procurement picture for the strategic deterrent force changed drastically. Once preliminary design of the air-breathing Blue Steel Mk 1 had been settled, the stand-off focus shifted towards a longer range Blue Steel Mark II with solid rocket boosters,

BLUE STEEL – METHOD OF DELIVERY

4. MINS AFTER RELEASE

RELEASE

TARGET

100 NM

RELEASE POINT FIX

RADAR FIX

RADAR FIX

Bristol Siddeley ramjets and a range of 800 miles. In addition, land and sea-based variants were discussed, and there was even a proposal for a manned Blue Steel to reach Mach 4.6. This 20-ton multi-stage rocket, to be mounted under the Vulcan, would have given Europe a novel means of putting satellites into low-earth orbits with a 560-lb payload.

However, the uprated Blue Steel Mk 2 was cancelled on 1 January 1960 in favour of the Douglas Skybolt air-launched ballistic missile projected to navigate over 1000 miles and deposit a two-megaton warhead within an accuracy of just hundreds of feet. Given that a Mk 2 V-bomber could carry two Skybolts, it was decided that 'the same deterrent threat as that represented by the force approved in August 1957' could be 'broadly achieved with 72 Mk 2 Vulcans, each carrying two Skybolts'. This reduced requirement offered the possibility of saving money for, 'if the airborne deterrent is to consist exclusively of Vulcans carrying Skybolt, the need for Victor B 2s will be limited to the number required for the interim Blue Steel force to contribute to the deterrent while the Vulcans are being modified to carry Skybolt, and for photographic reconnaissance'. On this basis, the Air Ministry estimated that the Mk 2 Victor order could be cut from 57 to 32.

Studies showed that Skybolt carriage on the low-slung Victor 'could only be achieved by some form of fin-folding' (there were eight of these). On the other hand, Handley Page was keen to claim aircraft/missile compatibility, and in July 1960 the company informed the Ministry of Aviation that the Victor B 2 could carry two Skybolts without modification to either aircraft or missile to improve ground clearance. Handley Page test pilot Philip Murphy flew Victor Blue Steel trials over Aberporth Range, and he recalls that 'the Victor/Skybolt combination was do-able'. The company claimed that adequate clearance had been obtained by mounting the missiles some 18 inches further forward, and that this position was satisfactory both structurally and aerodynamically.

In a letter to Air Minister George Ward on 21 June 1960, Sir Frederick said that 50 Victors could be modified as Skybolt carriers at a cost of 'well under £1 million'. The RAF Director of Operational Requirements reiterated that the number of Skybolts to be purchased – between 120-140 – could be carried by the planned frontline force of Vulcan B 2s, which meant saving the cost of developing and proving an installation on the Victor B 2, which might be difficult. He went on to explain that the issue of ensuring adequate ground clearance did not apply to the Vulcan or the B-52. Handley Page offered to install a new undercarriage to ensure adequate clearance, and 'you have my assurance', Sir Frederick declared on television in 1960, 'that the Victor 2 can carry Skybolt without needing either wing strengthening or undercarriage modification. Already it has flown with the equivalent

A Victor is marshalled back into its No 15 Sqn dispersal at RAF Cottesmore following the completion of a night mission

in weight and drag of two Skybolts under its wings'. He was referring to XA930 with its full drop tanks which approximated to two Skybolts, and trials demonstrated XA930's ability to land with only one drop tank in position.

Rumours about a possible cut in orders for Victor B 2s reached Fleet Street. *Daily Express* air correspondent Keith Thompson had discovered that 'the Victor, unlike the Vulcan, cannot easily be adapted to carry the American Skybolt air-launched rocket', and he wrote on 19 July 1960 that the 'half-completed project to strengthen the V-bomber force with 30 faster, higher-flying Victor 2s' was likely to be halted. On 25 July, the Defence Minister reiterated the position by saying that, if each Mk 2 Vulcan carried two Skybolts, the number of Mk 2 Victors in Bomber Command could be reduced without diminishing the V-force's deterrent capability, with a total capital saving of about £14 million over the next five years.

The decision to cut the Victor B 2 order by 25 was a bitter blow for Handley Page, although three (XL511-XL513) were quietly reinstated because so much work had been done on them that it would have cost nearly as much to recompense the company as to let them enter service. The whole UK aviation industry was then being rationalised, and negotiations for the takeover of Handley Page Ltd by the Hawker Siddeley Group were on the point of signature.

Contrary to the popular view, Sir Fred was well aware of the wisdom of joining a group while his company was out on a limb, and the Ministry still saw merit in the Victor programme within one of the groups. But the cancellation of the last 22 Victor B 2s (these had been slated to go to Nos 9 and 12 Sqns) undermined the price of Handley Page shares to the point where Hawker Siddeley would not pay what Sir Fred thought his company was worth. As only 34 Victor B 2s were produced in all, there were only enough aircraft initially free from trials work to equip Nos 100 and 139 Sqns at Wittering and the Victor Training Flight, which moved from Gaydon to Wittering in 1964 as the B 1/1A force wound down. Two Victor prototypes, 50 B 1s (of which 24 were converted to B 1As) and 34 B 2s came into existence. The Victor production line came to a halt with the delivery of XM718 to No 100 Sqn on 2 May 1963.

XM718, the last Victor to roll off the Handley Page production line, sits on display in No 100 Sqn colours at an airshow at RAF Wittering in the summer of 1963. This aircraft was later converted into an SR 2, and it served with No 543 Sqn and No 232 OCU prior to being struck off charge on 31 March 1976

COLOUR PLATES

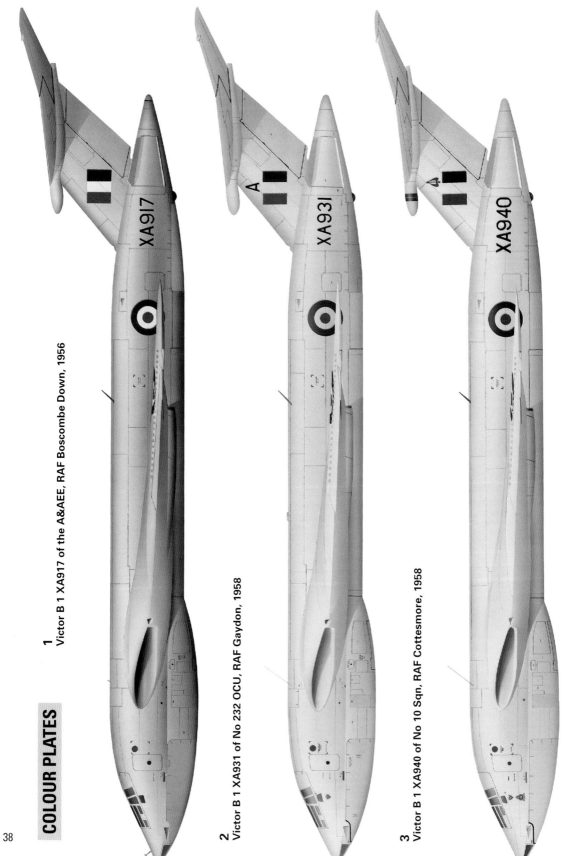

1
Victor B 1 XA917 of the A&AEE, RAF Boscombe Down, 1956

2
Victor B 1 XA931 of No 232 OCU, RAF Gaydon, 1958

3
Victor B 1 XA940 of No 10 Sqn, RAF Cottesmore, 1958

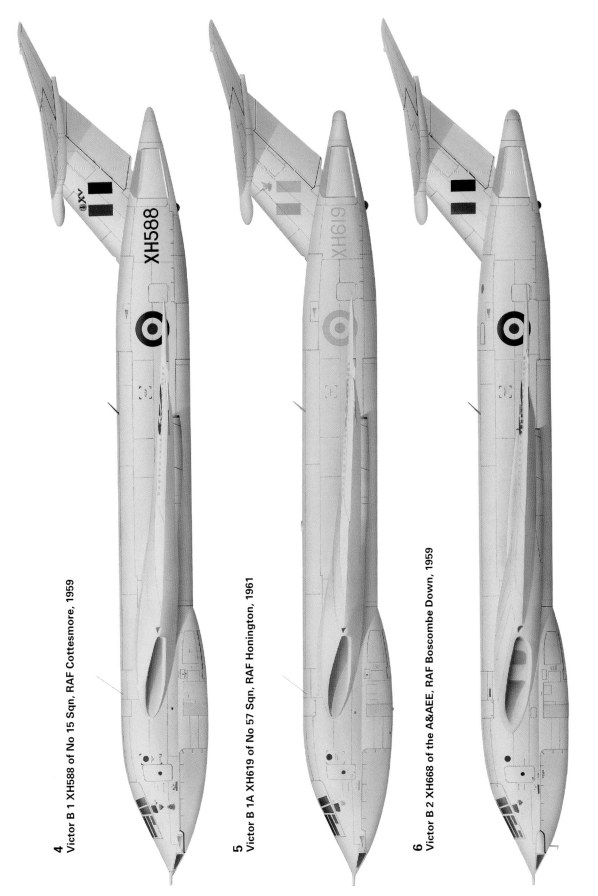

4
Victor B 1 XH588 of No 15 Sqn, RAF Cottesmore, 1959

5
Victor B 1A XH619 of No 57 Sqn, RAF Honington, 1961

6
Victor B 2 XH668 of the A&AEE, RAF Boscombe Down, 1959

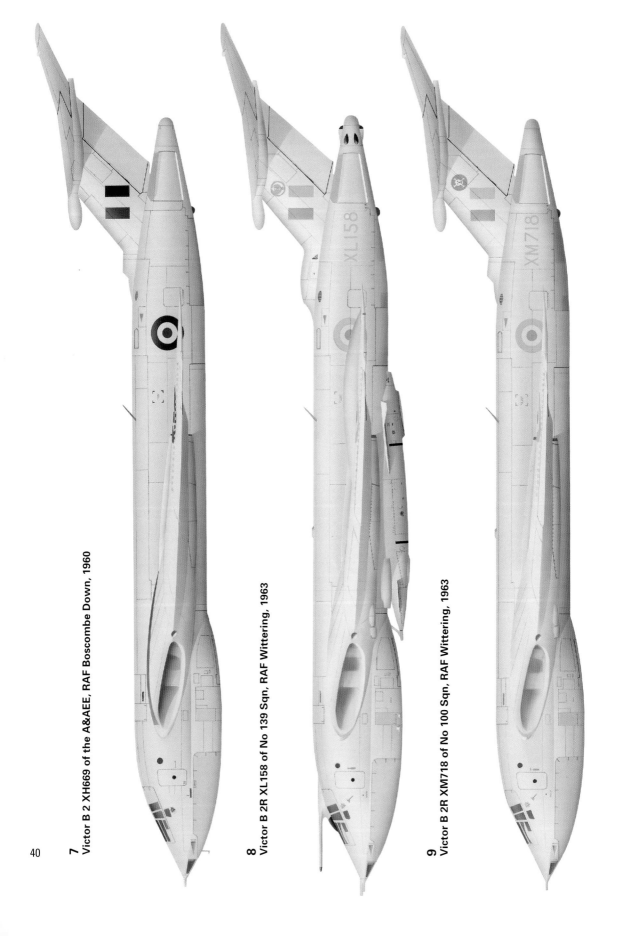

40

7
Victor B 2 XH669 of the A&AEE, RAF Boscombe Down, 1960

8
Victor B 2R XL158 of No 139 Sqn, RAF Wittering, 1963

9
Victor B 2R XM718 of No 100 Sqn, RAF Wittering, 1963

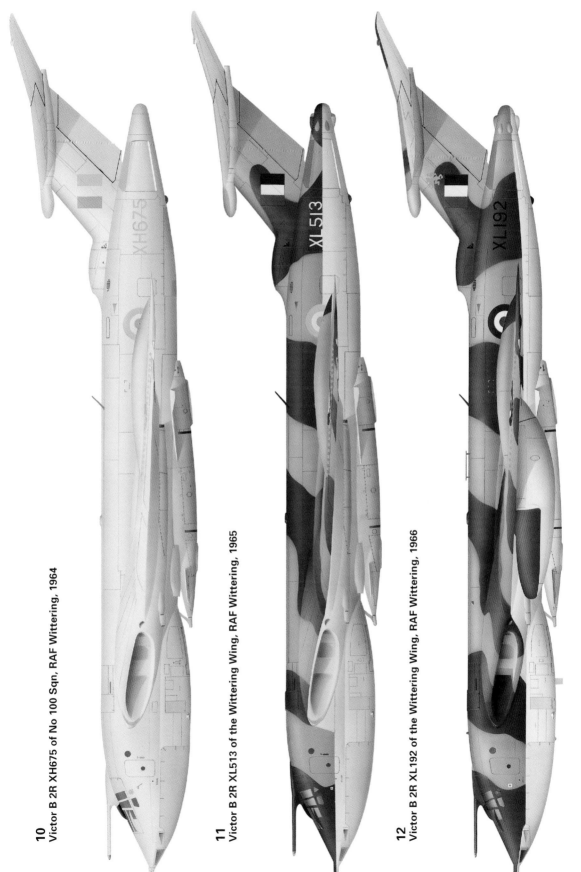

10
Victor B 2R XH675 of No 100 Sqn, RAF Wittering, 1964

11
Victor B 2R XL513 of the Wittering Wing, RAF Wittering, 1965

12
Victor B 2R XL192 of the Wittering Wing, RAF Wittering, 1966

41

13
Victor B 1A XH667 of the Honington Wing, RAF Honington, 1964

14
Victor B(SR) 2 XH672 of No 543 Sqn, RAF Wyton, 1969

15
Victor B 1 XA930 of the A&AEE, RAF Boscombe Down, 1961

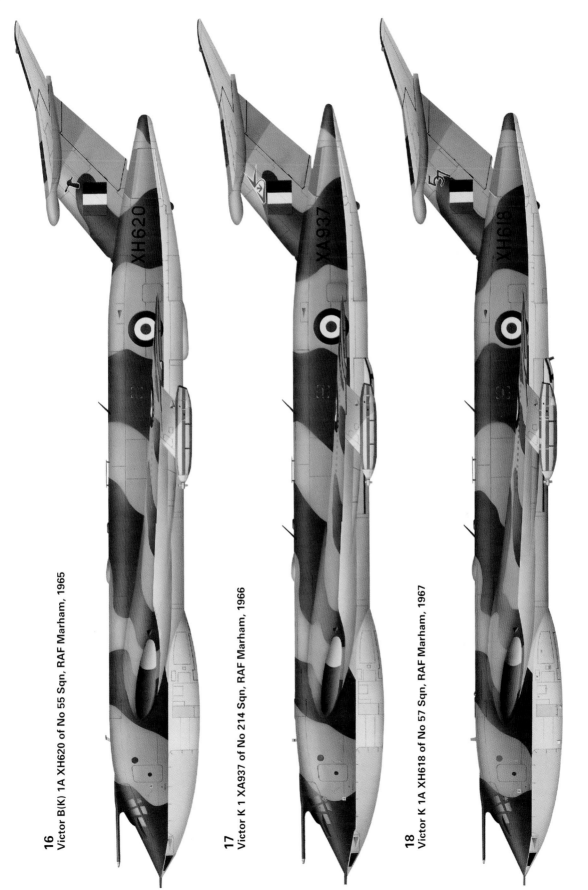

16
Victor B(K) 1A XH620 of No 55 Sqn, RAF Marham, 1965

17
Victor K 1 XA937 of No 214 Sqn, RAF Marham, 1966

18
Victor K 1A XH618 of No 57 Sqn, RAF Marham, 1967

43

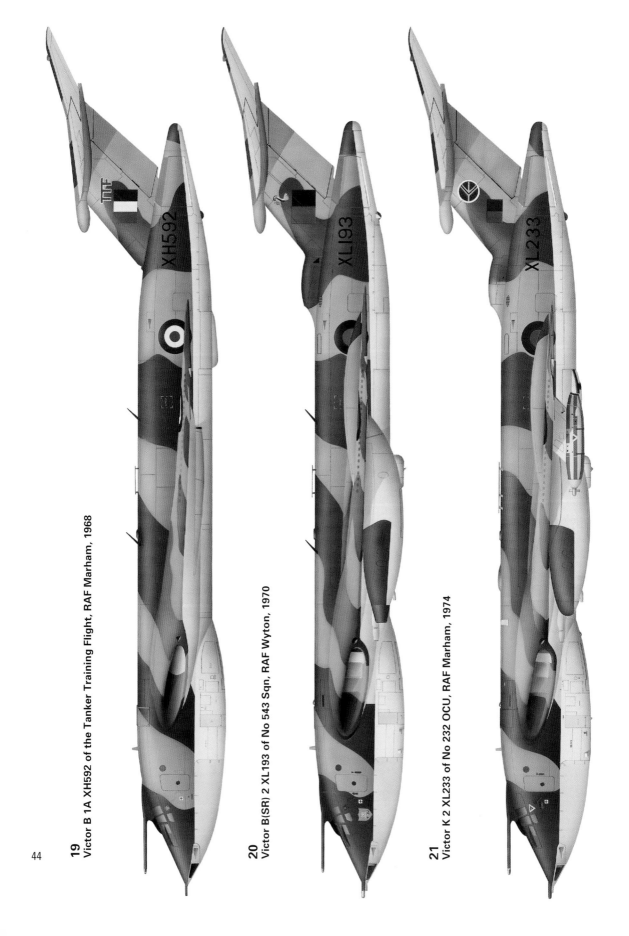

19
Victor B 1A XH592 of the Tanker Training Flight, RAF Marham, 1968

20
Victor B(SR) 2 XL193 of No 543 Sqn, RAF Wyton, 1970

21
Victor K 2 XL233 of No 232 OCU, RAF Marham, 1974

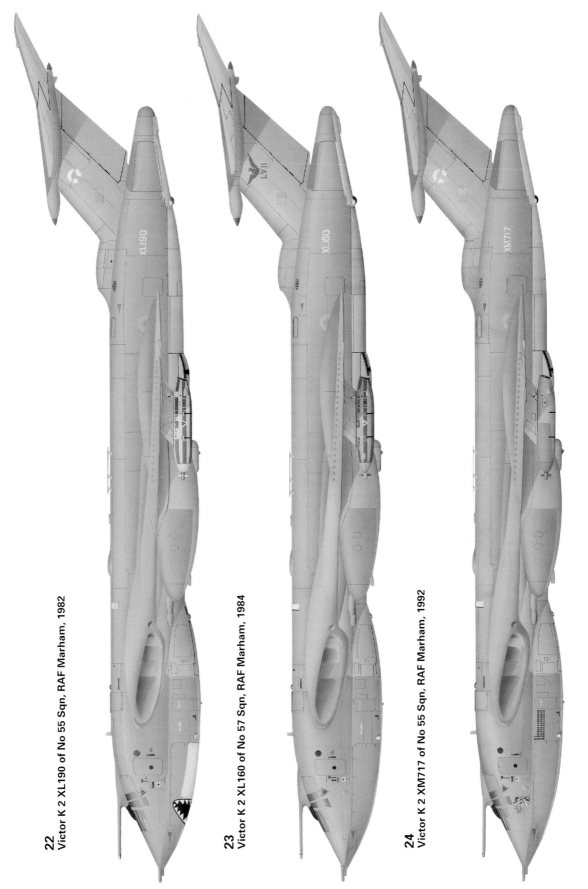

22
Victor K 2 XL190 of No 55 Sqn, RAF Marham, 1982

23
Victor K 2 XL160 of No 57 Sqn, RAF Marham, 1984

24
Victor K 2 XM717 of No 55 Sqn, RAF Marham, 1992

21
Victor K 2 XL233 of No 232 OCU, RAF Marham, 1974

18
Victor K 1A XH618 of No 57 Sqn, RAF Marham, 1967

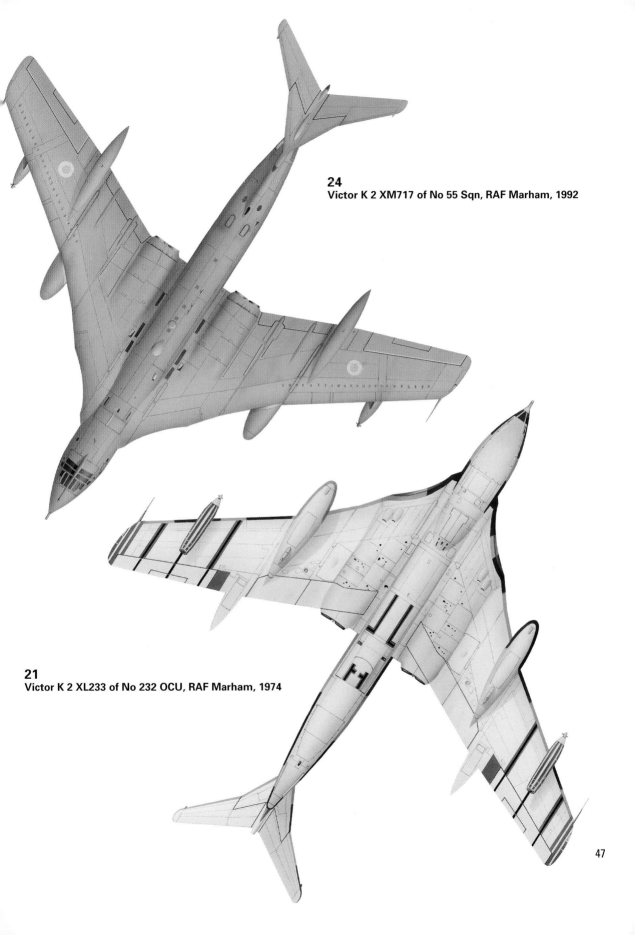

24
Victor K 2 XM717 of No 55 Sqn, RAF Marham, 1992

21
Victor K 2 XL233 of No 232 OCU, RAF Marham, 1974

DOWN TO EARTH

With the cancellation of Skybolt at the end of 1962, the RAF had to extend the operational life of the Mk 2 V-bomber/Blue Steel combination until the introduction of the Royal Navy's Polaris missile-equipped submarines at the end of the decade. By March 1963 this had been clarified to mean operating below the radar cover of the Soviet air defences, to provide 'a nuclear weapon which can be released from very low altitude, modifying Blue Steel to enable it to be launched from below 1000 ft and by improving the performance at low level of the bombing and navigation fit of the V-bombers'.

Beginning in March 1963, Aeroplane & Armament Experimental (A&AEE) Establishment at Boscombe Down undertook trials with Victor B 1A XH618 and a variety of B 2s 'to determine the capability of the aircraft for low-level operations, and to define appropriate techniques and limitations'. Sustained low-level flying at high temperatures from Khormaksar, in Aden, presented no handling problems, and the A&AEE was soon able to recommend clearance for RAF Victor low-level training up to 350 knots. 'It was found to be relatively easy to contour follow over the rolling terrain of southwest England by leaving the throttles at a fixed setting and accepting speed variations of 20 knots. In clear weather the forward view was adequate, but in rain the windscreen wipers were ineffective and the outlook deteriorated markedly. Lack of a terrain avoidance or follow system was an obvious shortcoming'.

Low-level crew training did not start until March 1963 because the weather during January and February had been exceptionally severe, with snow-and ice all over Britain. No 57 Sqn crews flew four low-level sorties at 1000 ft agl and then down to 500 ft agl. April 1963 saw No 55 Sqn starting low-level sorties, with Flt Lt D Mobberley and crew successfully flying the first on 29 April. No 55 Sqn was expected to be fully trained in low-level flying by the end of June 'to meet the Command's new policy'. In May 1963, No 10 Sqn commented in its Operational Record Book (ORB) that 'the squadron has now undertaken a low-level attack role. Due to

Bird's eye view of the classic Victor wing planform in 1960. The first four production Victors sported the standard RAF lightweight aluminium finish, but from XA921 onwards, they were coated in Titanine all-white anti-flash paint that was designed to reflect the intense heat-flash radiated by a nuclear explosion. Produced by Cellon, this gloss white paint was also used on Concorde.

aircraft fatigue limitations the majority of sorties are now undertaken at 1000 ft, with every third sortie at 500 ft agl. Low-level flying training took priority over all other flying during the month'.

Tony Davies was a No 10 Sqn co-pilot from August 1961 to December 1963, and he recalled;

'I distinctly remember the thrill of flying low level in this great white and beautiful bird for the first time in the spring of 1963. We descended over the Irish Sea and coasted into North Wales near Prestatyn. The moderately turbulent up- and down-drafts between the mountains and over the cols and valleys jolted the aircraft from time to time, and we actually flapped our wings in response! It was an exhilarating and almost wickedly defiant experience – the aircraft was never designed for low flying. It was 'Alice in Wonderland' stuff. As I flew along at 250 ft in the Victor B 1 I thought, "there is no way this beautiful shape should be doing this".'

On 3 May 1963 it was agreed that the Victor B 1/1A would be withdrawn from bomber service by mid-1965. A special British H-bomb designed for low-level release was eventually produced for the Vulcan and Buccaneer, but the weapon arrived far too late to save the B 1/1A crews at Cottesmore and Honington. They retained Yellow Sun 2 to the end, and the test crews at Boscombe Down concluded that the best means of B 1/1A delivery was to 'pop-up' just before target release, set a 'constant-attitude-climb' and lob the bomb off at a minimum safe height of 9000 ft.

Victors operated as singletons in the Mediterranean, on so-called *Lone-Ranger*s, and into North America on what were called *Oil-Burners* before the 1973 oil crisis. Out of Goose Bay, Labrador, they did much low flying over frozen terrain and from Offutt AFB, Nebraska, they flew over hot prairies and endless cereal crops, culminating in simulated attacks on targets such as the cross roads/grain silo seen in the Cary Grant film *North by North-West*.

Tony Davies' first contact with American soil was a 'crash' landing on the main runway at SAC HQ, Offutt AFB, on 2 May 1962 in XA929;

'The left brakes had become locked on after our departure from Goose Bay, unbeknownst to the crew, so we tobogganed down the centreline and ground the eight wheels on the left bogie down to half-circles. It speaks volumes for Handley Page and Dowty that when the RAF Unit at Offutt replaced the bogie and wheels, the retraction tests worked perfectly (with the aircraft up on jacks). There were no distortions and every micro-switch (three-greens, three-reds, lights out sequence) operated appropriately, together with the joyfully positive noises of doors "clunk" opening/closing and hydraulic legs winding up and down.'

The official view was that Mk 2 V-bombers 'are required to pose a measure of deterrence until at least 1970, and as such must be modified to enable them to operate in the low-level role against an increasing Soviet defence capability'. Hard on the heels of this decision came draft Air Staff Requirement No 1132 (Issue 4) – a new version of the original Blue Steel OR – which said that 'the Air Staff requires the further development of the Blue Steel missile to enable it to be launched from Mk 2 V-bombers flying at the lowest possible level in the height band 250 ft-1000 ft.'

On 1 July 1964 the Controller of Aircraft (CA) issued approval 'for the carriage, and launch in an emergency, of Blue Steel in the low-level launch role from Victor B Mk 2 aircraft'. Blue Steel firing trials were due to be completed by the end of the year, and he expected to offer 'a final CA Release, covering weapon effectiveness, accuracy, etc,' around March-April 1965. In November 1964, CA Release was amended to give clearance for filled and fuelled QRA, including flights to dispersal with operational warhead pods, by Victor B 2s.

In May-June 1964, an amended programme of modifications required for the V-bombers' low-level role were approved. It showed some changes from the original one in that it was not thought necessary to undertake work to improve the Victor's fatigue life, requirements for navigation system improvement were reduced and it was concluded that it would not be possible in the time available to obtain the special low-level ECM equipment at first envisaged. On the other hand, the proposed programme took account of extensive low-altitude flying trials, ground trials on the effect of bird strikes, work on the engines to give protection against bird strikes and to assess the effects of sustained low-level operations, installation of terrain warning equipment and the development of long-range fuel tanks.

The metal uppersurfaces of Victor B 2s were to be 'coloured by a variegated pattern of greys and greens', while undersurfaces could remain in the standard white anti-flash finish. Total estimated research and development costs of modifying the Mk 2 V-bombers for the low-level role were put at £2.2 million, and the estimated production cost about £11 million. Production costs of modifying Blue Steel for the low-level role were £0.25 million.

Of the 57 Blue Steels bought by the RAF, four were specifically for in-service proof firings by Bomber Command after the weapon's entry into service. The first of these proof firings, code-named Operation *Fresno*, took place from Victor B 2R XH673 of No 100 Sqn flying at 1000 ft asl and 350 knots IAS over the Aberporth Range on 27 May 1966. 'Its components functioned properly and it impacted within 1000 yards of the 25 nautical mile range target'. The second B 2 proof-firing was from XH675 of No 139 Sqn on 26 August, with the ORB noting that the weapon was 'launched at maximum range and landed 640 yards from the target.'

Low-level tactics swung the odds back in favour of the Victor force because there was no way that Soviet air defenders could cope with a coordinated low-level penetration from anywhere between the North Cape and the Black Sea. The V-bombers' operational mission was described as a high-low-high profile, and to conserve fuel, Victors would

John Moore of No 100 Sqn climbs out of XM716 somewhere sunnier than RAF Wittering. The windshield on the left of the cabin door was there to protect rear crew if they had to bail out. The much enlarged Conway engine air intakes of the Victor B 2 are clearly visible, as are kangaroo and kiwi 'zaps' to the left of the cabin door – the aircraft had clearly visited Australia and New Zealand during its time away from home

have transitted at height to a point just outside the forward extent of Soviet warning radar cover, where they would have descended. Once below 1000 ft, they would have been shielded by the earth's curvature from radar detection, and would have penetrated the vast Soviet coastline unopposed. No Soviet fighter of the time had an airborne radar that could look downwards and pick out a bomber among the ground returns below 5000 ft, so the opposing fighter pilot would have had to rely on eyesight alone. This would have been valueless at night, and even in daylight the amount of low cloud present on an average day in western Europe would have done little to assist the defences.

Operationally, low-level phases of up to 1000 nautical miles were originally envisaged 'in the extreme case', but in training they would normally be of the order of 350-500 nautical miles. A capability to operate in all weathers was required, the height at which aircraft would fly varying at the discretion of the captain according to prevailing conditions – it might be as low as 50 ft in good visibility or up to 1000 ft in poor visibility. Low-level flying training was to be conducted over the UK, North America and possibly North Africa, and the hazards peculiar to low-level flying – turbulence, impact damage (from hailstones and bird strikes), visibility and temperature – were spelt out. Pilot's Notes were amended 'to include advice on handling the airframe/engine combination at high speed/low level, including the pop-up manoeuvre where appropriate'.

Navigation and bombing equipment in the Victor was not unduly degraded by low-level flight down to 250 ft above ground level. In fact the low-level attack phase improved NBS weapon-aiming accuracy to 250 yards, and further refinement was possible because pilots could now map read and pass accurate fixes back to the navigation team.

The maximum all-up weight for the 'new' low-level optimised Victor B 2R was set at 223,000 lbs, and when crews were cleared down they found that the 'Küchemann carrots' were beneficial for low-level flight. The Green Satin Mk 2 and GPI Mk 6 navigation equipment were modified 'to function down to the lowest possible level'. All B 2Rs were equipped with the General Dynamics Terrain Following Radar (TFR), which was trialled by XL164 over the Libyan desert. The radar was housed in a cone on the Victor's nose, but the TFR device never proved effective and the B 2R force had to contour fly visually until the Wittering Wing disbanded.

After a series of low-level Blue Steel firings at Woomera had proved to be '100 per cent effective', the Wittering Wing became

The 'warty' ECM tail cone of Victor B 2R XL158. The technician on the ladder is looking through the back hatch into the rear equipment compartment where all manner of goodies, including the reserve brake parachute, could be stowed on overseas *Rangers*. The strakes on top of the airbrakes were there to improve efficiency

operational at low level in 1964. Modifications to individual missiles were not extensive, the main difference from before being that the two combustion chambers now fired together. However, release range was now reduced to 25-30 miles at low level instead of 200 miles high up, and when it was at release point the Victor had to climb sufficiently to give the missile room to fall away before it fired. The Blue Steel then zoomed to 17,000 ft, at which point the Stentor cut out, leaving the missile to detonate within a theoretical accuracy of 300 yards.

Once B 2Rs were cleared down to low-level, the radars of the SAM and anti-aircraft batteries were a much reduced threat. SAM sites had proliferated in the early 1960s, but they had been positioned to provide overlapping cover at height only. Consequently, there were great gaps in the low-level radar cover between the SAM sites through which the Victors could hope to pass undetected. An AEO would listen out for the searching SAM radars on his warning receiver and, as he could tell in which quadrant they were positioned, the pilot simply altered heading

XL513 at Radlett in its new low-level, glossy polyurethane camouflage. In all, 3222 Victor flights took place from Radlett before the airfield closed in 1970. The first Victor to be camouflaged, XL513 served with No 139 Sqn (twice), the Victor Training Flight and No 100 Sqn prior to being converted into a K 2. Subsequently issued to No 55 Sqn, XL513 spent time with No 232 OCU before returning to No 55 Sqn. It was written off at RAF Marham in a take-off accident on 28 September 1976

The crew chief talks to the pilot via an external intercom during engine start. The airman by the port wing is manning the fire extinguisher

to bypass the threat and the bomber was through the gap, leaving the SAM radar looking fruitlessly for an intruder that never came.

In fact the transition to low level left the Victor AEO with very little to do except to listen out for what was up ahead – to have used the jammers would only have given away the bomber's position. After years of spending millions of roubles perfecting a high-level defence system, the Soviets could mount no bigger threat against a Victor at low level than a soldier on the ground with a rifle. 'In the early days of low level', recalled one Wittering AEO, 'we went in fat, dumb and happy'.

A defender's problem was compounded still further when the uppersurfaces of all Victors were camouflaged in green and grey. XL513, the seventh aircraft to be converted into a B 2R, was the first to be so decked out when it returned from Radlett to No 139 Sqn in December 1963. When the press was invited to Wittering the following February, XL513 stood out among its all-white brethren in the words of one observer 'like a one-armed bandit in a Salvation Army hall'. It made a searing take-off with its Blue Steel snuggled marsupial-fashion.

On 21 September 1964, *The Times'* defence correspondent described a low-level sortie in Victor XL190 of No 100 Sqn;

'At Wittering, one of the operational bases of No 3 Group, RAF Bomber Command, a Victor bomber of No 100 Sqn, commanded by Sqn Ldr C A Herbert and armed with a Blue Steel nuclear missile, took off last week with its crew of five – and with me helmeted, oxygen-masked and strapped firmly into the No 6 seat wondering whether all this was not carrying the search for truth a shade too far.

Wg Cdr Harry Archer, officer commanding No 100 Sqn (kneeling far left), poses with the Downey and Goodman crews on 22 August 1967 prior to their departure for an air display in Toronto. The winged Lawrence Minot Trophy (foreground) was awarded in the annual Anglo-American Bombing and Navigation Competition, and it had been won by No 100 Sqn the previous March. It had been awarded to No 57 Sqn in 1965 and 1966. Harry Archer had served previously as a test pilot in the US flying, among other things, the U-2

Also seen in 1967, this No 139 Sqn crew consisted of, from left to right, Rod King (Co-pilot), Pete Kibble (Nav Plotter), Tom Barnard (Captain), Ralph Devereux (Nav Radar) and Alan Farmer (AEO) (*Tom Barnard*)

'The RAF's intention was to demonstrate conclusively that the low-flying V-bomber is not, as some observers have suggested, just an air staff fantasy. AM Sir John Grandy, Air Officer Commanding-in-Chief, Bomber Command, like all his officers and men, is convinced that their newly perfected flying techniques will prolong the effective life of the V-bomber force well into the 1970s.

'Suggestions that new developments in radar and in air defence measures such as barrage balloons and infantry anti-aircraft missiles might make the low-flying bomber and its successor, the TSR 2, obsolete almost before they were fully operational were completely discounted. The view of staff officers and senior commanders in the V-bomber force is that the problem of effective defence against fast, low-flying aircraft is far from being overcome.

'Although there have been difficulties and delays in the development of the TSR 2, the RAF believe that when it comes into squadron service it will be an essential part of Britain's nuclear striking force, whatever other delivery systems may be introduced. The low-flying methods to which the V-bomber force have now been almost completely converted will be made much simpler by the advanced radar and electronic equipment of the TSR 2.

'The flight preliminaries, carried out by the aircraft captain with the help of an RAF doctor, included much blood-chilling information on how the parachute might be persuaded to open in time in the event of anyone's having to abandon the aircraft less than 1000 ft above the ground – and alternatively how to get a quick ration of oxygen if the same thing happened a little nearer to outer space.

'The lavish non-alcoholic meal in the aircrew mess had a hearty condemned-cell solicitude about it. At 1431 hrs exactly, the crew chief on the runway disconnected his communication line to the aircraft, and with it had gone the last contact with the reassuring ordinariness of people who live habitually on the ground.

'With a haste that seemed disrespectful to one brought up on the barley-sugar routine of civil flying, the four jet engines started simultaneously. Victor XL190 moved along the runway, and in less time than it takes to say independent deterrent it was climbing apparently vertically into the air, with at least one of its occupants already seriously in need of oxygen.

'Within four minutes the Victor was cruising, if such a word can fairly be applied to such a precipitate vehicle, at 21,000 ft. One of the first tasks was to test the accuracy of the Blue Steel missile, which was found to have an error of half-a-mile that would have to be corrected in flight before it could be launched. Apart from that the only event of note on the high-level part of the flight was a 360-degree turn that took the bomber with great precision through its own slipstream, bringing mocking congratulations from the captain to the co-pilot at the controls.

A Victor B 2R of No 100 Sqn dominates the static display area at an unnamed airfield during a public display. The unit crest has disappeared from the fin because in March 1964 Nos 100 and 139 Sqn Victors were pooled to form the Wittering Wing, to which was added Victor Training Flight aircraft after their move from Cottesmore. Thereafter, Victors were centrally serviced, and crews were allocated aircraft from the central pool

A B 2R lands and streams while an RAF Wessex helicopter crew stands and watches. The fully extended Victor airbrakes were copied on the Blackburn Buccaneer

'At Edinburgh the aircraft turned south to begin the low-level section of the flight. From the Tweed to the imaginary target area in Lincolnshire the bomber followed the contours, flying at 300 knots at about 250 ft over deafened villagers and almost within milking distance of cows which looked, even if they were not, enormously impressed.

'Passing between, and apparently slightly below, Harrogate and Leeds, the flight had settled into a smooth and efficient routine. On the intercommunication set the only sounds were the breathing of the crew, the regular height checks being read from the radar altimeter and periodic readings of time and distance.

'At 1625 hrs the simulated launch of the Blue Steel missile took place, its accuracy computed by a radar aiming point on the ground. A rough check by the crew estimated that it would have fallen 20 yards west and 60 yards south of the target – near enough, as the plotter said, to make them catch their breath. Ten minutes later the crew were back at base being debriefed and interrogated on the mission.

'This high-low technique would enable the V-bombers to fly at their best operational height until they came within range of enemy early warning radar defences, and then to come down and take advantage of the screening effect of the earth's curve. As senior officers of Bomber Command repeatedly insisted, the effectiveness of the method is nothing to do with whether Britain has an independent deterrent or not. It is simply one of the most effective ways of doing what they have been told to do.

'The technical doubts about flying low and fast in aircraft designed to fly in the rare atmosphere at great heights have been largely dispelled. Scientists at the Royal Aircraft

Camouflage evolution – XL513 has its serial number applied in white . . .

. . . while this aircraft has had it painted on in black so as to minimise detection still further

Establishment at Farnborough have assured the RAF that the fatigue life of the V-bombers, some of which have been strengthened for the new role, is tough enough to enable them to carry out all the training that is necessary for the aircrew.

'In operations, the staffs say, the bombers would fly faster and lower than they do in training. Whatever the views of strategists about the nuclear striking force, Bomber Command crews are convinced that they will be able to get through for some years unless there is some startling advance in the Soviet surface-to-air defences.

'Whatever doubts there may be about this in the minds of independent observers, one thing is certain. There can be few military organisations in the world more dedicated and efficient than Bomber Command. The aircrew, the staffs and the supporting technicians have the confident, relaxed air of the highly trained professional. There can be little doubt that by their application to the demanding techniques of low-level attack they have succeeded in extending the life of the V-bomber, even if in demonstrating it they have measurably shortened mine.'

A Wittering QRA crew dash from their Standard Vanguard (which was always kept on a battery charger) to their waiting aircraft on the ORP overlooking the Great North Road. The Crew Chief, standing far right, is ready and waiting for a rapid engine start

After describing Bomber Command's alert and readiness posture, AM Grandy said that there were six factors on which the penetration of enemy airspace depended – aircraft performance, evasive routeing, high or low-level capability, ECM, the success of earlier strikes in destroying enemy

'Scramble' – four Victors roar off in quick succession from the ORP on 27 November 1964

defences and stand-off weapons. Bomber Command deployed them all in 1964, and after a tantalising glimpse of a map of the USSR with a line extending 1350 miles from Murmansk in the north to Odessa in the South, the C-in-C said that the V-force could penetrate that line anywhere, or fly round the ends.

Going low-level gave Bomber Command 'an expanded range of options'. With a maximum high-level speed of Mach 0.92, a low-level capability up to 1500 nautical miles and a low-level dash speed in excess of 400 knots, the Victor B 2R underlined Sir John's conclusion that, 'penetration by aircraft of Bomber Command of areas covered by the most modern and sophisticated air defence systems could not be successfully prevented'. It all confirmed the Chief of Air Staff's observation on the Victor in 1957. 'I would say it is probably better for the specific task which it has been built for than anything in the world'.

Blue Steel began to be phased-out of service during the last quarter of 1968 as Polaris took over the strategic deterrent. The Missile Engineering Squadron at RAF Wittering had disbanded by the end of March 1968, followed by No 100 Sqn on 1 October and No 139 Sqn on 31 December. The QRA aircraft on the ORP alongside the A1 were towed away for the last time, and for the Victor force the nuclear weapons delivery phase of the Cold War was over.

The last Victor QRA crew, together with the RAF policemen (with white caps) and Alsatian who guarded the armed aircraft '24/7', pose for a photograph on 31 December 1968. Sitting on top of the No 139 Sqn QRA car are Dave Weir (Nav Plotter) and Ian Thompson (Co-pilot), while standing, from left to right, are Geoff Thomas (Captain), Vic Pheasant (AEO) and Chris Ferris (Nav Radar). They are wearing blue QRA armbands. The crew had asked if they could go off-state at noon on the 31st so that they could attend the New Year party in the Officers' Mess, but Group replied that they had to stay on until midnight. So No 139 Sqn planned a ceremonial 'coming off state' at midnight, with a Blue Steel missile trolley towing the crew round to the Mess! Group got wind of it and said that 'on second thoughts' they could come off state at midday (*Vic Pheasant*)

SHOWING THE FLAG

Because the Victor was both highly visible and had the range and speed to stride the globe, it contributed to British prestige in two ways – by impressing friends and by overawing adversaries. In the cause of friendship, three Victors from No 139 'Jamaica' Sqn would smoke-trail green, yellow and black Jamaican national colours over the Kingston stadium, where the Commonwealth Games were held in 1966. But if less convivial surroundings beckoned, the Victor's secondary role, as laid down in June 1954, was to 'supplement tactical bomber forces if the need arises by delivering maximum weight of High Explosive bombs by night, and if practicable by day, on targets at relatively short distance from base'.

The Victor's conventional bomb load was awesome. Back in 1947, the V-bomber specification had called for a total bomb capacity of 20,000 lbs, made up of one Blue Danube, or two 10,000-lb conventional bombs or 81,000 lbs of munitions. At the time it was thought that the nuclear weapon might be six feet in diameter and up to 30 ft long, and although Blue Danube eventually turned out to be much smaller than this, the initial stimulus resulted in a truly cavernous HP 80 bomb-bay – 34 ft long, 9 ft wide and 7 ft deep – that was some five feet longer than that of the Avro Vulcan. The Victor bomb-bay was theoretically big enough to accommodate, as an alternative to the bulky Blue Danube, one 22,000-lb 'Grand Slam', two 12,000-lb 'Tallboys', four 10,000-lb bombs or no fewer than 48 1000-lb bombs or 39 2000-lb Type 2 mines. All bomb loading was done by vehicle-mounted hydraulic jacks, making pits or ramps unnecessary. One 10,000-lb bomb could be loaded in ten minutes, while a full load of 48 1000-lb bombs took only 30 minutes.

Bob Prothero and his No 100 Sqn crew overfly RAF Wittering. Bob was the last pilot to get airborne in a Victor when XM715 inadvertently lifted off while undertaking a high speed taxi run at Bruntingthorpe on 3 May 2009

Armed with a Blue Steel training round, an anonymous B2R is seen in its element at dusk

B 2R XL231 powers skyward. The 'Whitcomb' bodies can be seen protruding from the trailing edges just outboard of the flaps. This aircraft served with No 139 Sqn, the Wittering Wing and the Victor Training Flight prior to being converted into a K 2 by Hawker Siddeley at Woodford. Subsequently assigned to No 57 Sqn (twice), No 232 OCU and No 55 Sqn, XL231 was retired to the Yorkshire Air Museum at Elvington on 25 November 1993. It is one of just five complete examples of the Victor remaining today

In addition, Handley Page designed underwing bomb carriers, although they were never manufactured. Each was 45 ft long, with a ten foot-span tailplane and 20 ft-long bomb doors, and they would have increased the Victor's load of 1000-lb bombs to a phenomenal 76. If they had ever been built and fitted, 'Hazel' Hazelden remembers thinking that the Victor would have been just able to fly from London to Manchester and back. In the end, the RAF restricted the Victor to 35 1000-lb bombs, but this was still 14 more than the Vulcan could stow.

Iron bombs were loaded in groups of four or seven on to septuple carriers before being brought out to a Victor. There were seven loading points in the bomb-bay. Those carriers at loading points 2 and 5 were attached to the bomb-bay, roof while those at loading points 1, 4 and 6 were suspended some 30 inches below from special adaptors to stagger release – loading point 3 was reserved for a 10,000-lb weapon. Bombs on the carriers could be released individually, in groups or all together via the '90-Way' Bomb Control Installation which, as its name implied, allowed crews to drop weapons in a variety of combinations and at any timing spacing up to ten seconds. Electric pulses initiated the sequencing, but no bomb could be released until the one below it had gone.

The Victor's retracting bomb-bay doors were designed so as not to disturb the airflow along the fuselage, but they were so effective that the smooth airflow prevented bombs from making a clean exit. Air deflector plates had therefore to be fitted to the front end of the Victor bomb-bay. Similar to the gills of a radial engine, they were lowered automatically when the doors opened and retracted when they closed. Breaking up the airflow entering the bomb-bay, they reduced the pressure build-up when the doors were opened.

Bombing trials with XA921 were completed in June 1959 when 35 1000-lb bombs were dropped successfully. All Victors were now cleared for conventional release from 14,000 ft upwards, although

for extended range the bomb load was reduced to 21,000 lbs, plus a forward bomb-bay tank at loading point 1. There was a senior officer who flung his Victor around so much at low level in the Far East that the front bomb-bay was torn out.

High-level visual bomb delivery had distinct limitations over cloud-covered northern Europe, but in warmer climates it could be more precise than radar bombing, especially against low-radar-response targets such as jungle lairs. The Victor specification had called for a visual bombing station readily accessible from the navigation station. From his prone position in the nose, the Nav Plotter had a clear field of view ten degrees aft of the vertical to the horizontal forward. The Nav Radar brought the aircraft in towards the target using his H2S, and the Plotter would initiate release at up to 54,000 ft using the T4 visual bombsight into which were fed Green Satin outputs of drift and groundspeed.

Victor crews periodically refined their conventional bombing skills over Libyan ranges and aircraft detached to Butterworth on Exercise *Profiteer* every year after the Malayan Emergency. Although they did nothing more aggressive than drop bombs on the Song Song and China Rock ranges, they were there not so much to go into action as to be seen to be in a position to do so. 'We were not sure what we were there for because we had no targets', said a No 10 Sqn pilot, but when B 1s flew round US bases in the Philippines they were demonstrating that Britain had not lost the will, or the capability, to defend the Commonwealth.

To make a point XH648, flown by Flt Lt 'Tommy' Thompson and his Cottesmore crew, dropped 35 1000-lb bombs for the benefit of the Far Eastern press. Fortunately, none of the observers appreciated the crew's fear that when the proximity fuse set off the bottom bomb in the stick, it might initiate a chain reaction running back up to the aircraft itself. Suffice to say that their worries were groundless and the crew heard the bombs explode one by one.

B 1A XH648 of No 15 Sqn, flown by Flt Lt 'Tommy' Thompson and his crew, unleashes its 35,000-lb bomb load over Malaysia's Song Song weapons range. As can been seen from the deposition pattern, the Victor's septuple carrier held bombs in clusters of seven at five loading points. The electrical system was configured in such a way that no upper bomb on the carrier could be released until those directly below it had fallen away. A veteran of service with Nos 57 (thrice), 15 and 55 Sqns, as well as No 232 OCU and the Tanker Training Flight, XH648 is the oldest surviving Victor. Converted into a K 1A in the late 1960s via Modification 4170, the aircraft was retired to IWM Duxford on 2 June 1976

A pilot instructor from No 232 OCU looks down through the optically flat glass of the Victor's visual bomb aiming position. Operationally, the Nav Radar directed the target run-in from his H2S and the bombs were dropped by the Nav Plotter lying prone in the visual bombing position. The tube protruding from the tip of the nose supplied pressure during flight to the bellows of the powered flying control artificial feel system

Tony Davies recalled;

'We deployed en masse to Butterworth, just abeam Penang Island, in Malaysia, to play our part in Confrontation. There was much practice bombing on Song Song, an islet just south of Penang which was reputedly inhabited by Komodo dragons, plus some flying visits to Singapore and exercises over the South China Sea. These latter exercises ended with a wide frontal attack from the east on Kuala Lumpur and north Malaysia, during which we were able to outwit the defending RAAF Sabres (based at Butterworth) by flying above their ceilings, having cruise climbed for hours to above 50,000 ft.'

Although Tengah, in Singapore, was developed as a Class 1 airfield with a nuclear weapon storage area, it was the V-force with iron bombs that provided strategic reassurance after 16 September 1963, when a newly independent Malaysia came under threat from Indonesia. During the Indonesian Confrontation period (December 1963-August 1966), V-bombers were among the forces earmarked to reinforce the Far East Air Force (FEAF). Indonesian 'Badger' bombers began to probe nightly to within five miles of Singapore before turning back, and Operation *Addington* envisaged V-bombers being positioned to be ready to eliminate Indonesian air force capabilities if they launched air attacks against Malaysia or Singapore in riposte for Commonwealth action against paramilitary bases mounting infiltrations.

There were three aspects to the Victors' task during Confrontation – rapid deployment to the Far East, detachment at Tengah or Butterworth and possible operations against Indonesian targets from RAAF Darwin or Labuan. Under Operation *Chamfrom*, arrangements were made in December 1963 to airlift servicing parties and spares pack-ups in support of four Victors from Honington and Cottesmore. Later that month, four No 15 Sqn B 1As flew out to Tengah and then in early January 1964, this quartet moved to Butterworth. Crews were rotated back to the UK in February, and No 15 Sqn B 1As continued at Butterworth until 30 September 1964, when they handed over to Vulcan B 2s of No 12 Sqn.

In parallel with the No 15 Sqn deployment, four B 1As from No 55 Sqn flew out to Tengah from Honington, and this commitment was taken over by No 57 Sqn from 17 October 1964. The No 57 Sqn Operational Record Book (ORB) noted that 'the first flight made by each crew was a familiarisation with the local area, including the circuits of RAAF Butterworth and RAF Changi. There was only one profile, and the majority of the other flights were bombing at Song Song and China Rock ranges'. Nos 10 and 15 Sqns disbanded as Victor units in March and October 1964, respectively, following the arrival of all Victor B 2Rs into service, leaving Honington's B 1As and their crews responsible for the Far East rotation.

As an illustration of crew rotation during *Chamfrom* detachments, the No 55 Sqn ORB for May 1964 recorded that 'Flt Lt Farlam and his crew left Honington on the 12th to replace Flt Lt Gallienne and his crew, who returned on the 21st. Wg Cdr Houston left Honington with his crew on the 20th to take over command of the det from Sqn Ldr Brettell.'

'No 55 Sqn was involved in an alert exercise based on the scenario that hostile aircraft would make a dawn attack on the airfield on the 12 March. To counter this, two Victors were prepared for take-off before dawn on

6.5-hour flights so as to be off the airfield during the strike. The two other Victors were loaded with 21 x 1000-lb HE bombs and put on 20-minute readiness. The four aircraft were dispersed about the airfield. The exercise was terminated at 0900 hrs on 12 March.'

It was at 1700 hrs on 24 November 1964 that Flt Lt Terry Filing and his No 57 Sqn crew departed Tengah in XH614. They were scheduled for a five-hour trip with eight 100-lb practice bombs, and the initial climb was going well as the Victor entered a rain cloud at 14,000 ft. Suddenly, as it passed 23,000 ft, there was a loud bang and a bright flash. The crew's first reaction was that they had been struck by lightning, but then the No 1 engine started to run down rapidly, and even though there was no fire warning indication, a bright orange glow was reflected from the cloud. Flt Lt Filing immediately initiated the fire drill, closing down Nos 1 and 2 engines as he did so, and turned back towards Singapore.

After some 15 seconds the orange glow died, and it was assumed that the fire had gone out. Then 15 seconds later there was a second bang followed by indications that No 3 engine had failed. Again the fire warning light did not illuminate, but this time there was no orange glow. While the co-pilot and AEO concentrated on switching and aligning the electrics to the one remaining engine, Terry Filing had to consider the situation quickly. Two engines appeared to have blown up violently, a third had been flamed out, probably damaged by the explosion, and although the one remaining Sapphire appeared to be serviceable, it did not leave much in reserve. Filing therefore decided to aim for land and re-light the No 2 engine. If that succeeded then he would try and land the Victor. If not, then the crew would bail out.

At 12,000 ft, in the descent, the Victor broke cloud some 37 miles from base. With 95 per cent set on the starboard outer engine, height was being lost at 500-800 ft per minute, so it seemed a good time to try and re-light the No 2 engine at 10,000 ft. On the fourth attempt it started.

By now the B 1A was at 6000 ft, and with two engines turning, a visual circuit and low speed idling check were carried out. After a final approach at 170 knots, the Victor touched down 200 ft past the runway threshold at 158 knots. The brake parachute was streamed and the aircraft came to rest 20 yards from the end of the runway with no other damage. For this 'exceptional feat of leadership, airmanship and courage', Flt Lt Filing was awarded the Air Force Cross.

Post-flight examination revealed that both Nos 1 and 3 engines had disintegrated. Severed fuel lines had caused the fire in No 1 engine, but the orange glow had been the only indication because the fire warning system had also been severed by the explosion. Although the Sapphire engine was generally very reliable in the Far East, XH614 had fallen foul of a tropical phenomenon known as 'centreline closure'. When flying on full power, the blades of the Sapphire compressor were at maximum stretch, with the minimum of blade clearance. If the

This Victor B 1A in low level camouflage is surrounded by its 'limited war' load of 35 1000-lb bombs. One of the most crucial, if rarely appreciated, roles throughout the life of the V-force was that of the RAF Policeman, who safeguarded the bombers and their weapons both night and day

engine then entered a tropical rainstorm, the injection of super-cooled water caused the compressor casing to cool more rapidly than the rotor. This reduced the clearance of the blade tips still further until they struck the casing with catastrophic results.

The cure for 'centreline closure' on Victor B 1s was either to increase compressor blade tip clearances or redesign the inside of the engine so that it could accept contact between the casing and the blade tips. As the former would reduce compressor efficiency, the inside of the Sapphire casing was coated with an abrasive ceramic. This not only reduced the rate of heat loss, and thereby the differential between casing and blade cooling rates, but also if contact was made the blade tips would be ground away slightly so that the engine did not disintegrate. It was a good 'fix', although centreline closure never went away for the B 1 force. On 1 April 1971, whilst transiting from RAF Gan to Tengah at an altitude of 43,000 ft, Victor tanker XH591 of No 55 Sqn was engulfed by a cumulo-nimbus cloud which caused centreline closure of all four engines. Speedy action by the crew enabled three engines to be re-started and the crew flew on to Singapore without further mishap.

Robert R Rodwell of *Flight* magazine witnessed the No 57 Sqn training programme from the sixth seat of B 1A XH621 while operating out of Tengah in early 1965;

'Fleetingly, I saw a junk through the forward windscreen, before losing it behind the co-pilot's head. Then our gentle descent from 2000 ft was over. We had turned to starboard and were running in for the coast. There was nothing but the scatter of tiny islands, vast expanses of yellow sand – the tide was out – and a neat green cultivated littoral with wooded hills behind. Aboard XH621 at this low altitude the air-conditioning system was fighting a losing battle with Malaysian heat and the encumbrances with which contemporary military aviators (and their guest) are hung.

'The forward-facing Crew Chief's seat in the Victor is an advance on that in the Vulcan – one has an outside view. The Nav Plotter behind was calling out our safety height – 4800 ft – for this low-level leg. Needless to say, our actual height was only a fraction of this. Although it was made clear before take-off that the speeds and heights at which we were to fly were not necessarily representative of Bomber Command's low-level techniques, I was pledged not to mention them. We had flown out from Tengah at 2000 ft and 250 knots and had descended substantially for this low-level run, but more specific than that I must not be.

'This brief experience of low-level flight, thrown in during a medium level visual bombing mission over the Song Song range off the coast of northwest Malaysia, was to prove adequately that a large V-bomber can be flown through a contour-hugging pattern at a moderate speed. It left one ready to accept that the contours would be even more closely hugged, and the speed somewhat less moderate, in an operational mission.

'The coastal plain gave way to undulating country. The Nav Plotter, Sqn Ldr W Milne, No 57 Sqn detachment commander at RAF Tengah, was already calling out instructions. "You're 300 yards to the right of track" – later, "Starboard, two miles ahead, a spot height, 730 ft, that's the highest ground for about 20 miles". The spot height, a lonely, jutting fang of a tree-clad rock like a small green Gibraltar, disappeared from view behind the captain's head.

'Undulating country was left behind. Now we were coming to some grown-up hills. Directly ahead a wooded minor mountain, reaching 2000 ft or so, assumed Himalayan proportions. My sangfroid cracked a bit and sweat ran free, but the Victor gently rose, the green slopes slipped away and then we were over the top with a few hundred feet to spare and gently going down the other side. "Just missed a birdstrike then", the co-pilot remarked.

'When the 22-minute low-level run ended, the Victor began its climb to height for the main business of the day. A series of checks were made as the aircraft passed through 10,000 ft. After that we levelled off at 26,500ft to keep below a layer of cirrus cloud and skirted the edge of a massive cloud build-up over the Malaysian coast. Flat Aussie accents coming up over the R/T left no doubt about the proprietorship of Butterworth, the base which we were now working with, or the range control at Song Song.

'The Nav Plotter squeezed past to crawl into the prone visual bombing position in the nose, and for the next two hours a pair of shoes, heels up, was all that could be seen of him. We had eight 100-lb practice bombs to drop from heights a little over 30,000 ft. Each time the run was made from 17 to 20 miles out at 295 knots IAS and 450 knots groundspeed.

'The target, I was told, was a large fluorescent raft. The run-in patter varied only in detail on each successive run – instructions from navigator to pilot interspersed with acknowledgements. "Right, right, right, steady, wings level. Three-and-a-half miles from release. Bombs selected. Steady, steady. Bomb doors open". There was a slight cobblestone effect as the doors opened and the smooth airflow over the belly was disturbed, the instrument panels beginning to shimmy on their mountings. Then a "Steady" litany of increasing frequency from the navigator, broken with "Bomb gone". Moments later, by leaning far forward for a craning look back, he could see it fall, and called out "Bomb away". The pilot closed the bomb-bay doors, and several times the navigator, watching for the burst, was able to give a rough assessment of the bomb's range and bearing from the target before the accurate figures were "sung sung" over

Victor B 1 XA928 of No 10 Sqn flies low over a Malaysian fishing village in 1960. This aircraft would be converted into a K 1 tanker in 1964 and subsequently serve with Nos 57 and 214 Sqns prior to being struck off charge on 16 December 1976

the R/T by the range control as a three-character code group. Then it was back to base down the Malacca Straits.'

The nearest Victors ever came to bombing in anger was in September 1964. In the words of the No 55 Sqn ORB;

'At the beginning of the month relations between Indonesia and Malaysia deteriorated. Night flying was cancelled and a day training sortie recalled. Operational generation of aircraft was started. No 55 Sqn Victors and other Tengah-based aircraft were dispersed on the airfield. Victors XH649 and XH594 were prepared with 14 x 1000-lb bombs and fuel and given Combat Ready checks. They were allocated to Flt Lt E J Randell and crew and Flt Lt R J Russell and crew, who had completed briefing on targets and were flight-planned for rapid dispersal to Gan. Victors XH645 and XH646 were prepared for dispersal without bomb loads. All crews were brought to one hour's readiness.'

From 3 to 8 September crew readiness was maintained at one hour and air raid shelters, sited on large monsoon ditches, were constructed with timber and sand bags near the dispersed aircraft, barrack block and squadron offices. From 10 September crew readiness was relaxed to three hours; three days later, the squadron commander and specialist leaders went to HQ FEAF for a conference and were introduced to a new plan, for which target study and flight planning then began. On 16 September 'Flt Lt R J Russell and crew and Flt Lt Bissell and crew were dispersed to RAAF Butterworth in their Victors with target Go-Bags and side arms'.

This alert posture lasted nearly all month. From 22 to 26 September, 'the readiness was relaxed to 17 hours, with bombs removed from the aircraft. Limited training sorties were flown by all crews during this period, in order to regain flying efficiency'. Then on 27 September 'the readiness was relaxed to 48 hours and the dispersed aircraft returned to Tengah. It was now possible for normal training to be resumed.'

As tensions eased, No 57 Sqn Victors were sent to participate in Exercise *Hot Squirrel* from 3 to 5 February 1965 'to test the fighter defences of northern Australia and to familiarise crews with operating from Darwin'. Transit was in darkness, 'the aircraft taking off from Tengah at midnight and arriving at Darwin at dawn'. Four Victors were involved, an extra crew and groundcrew flying to Australia in a Transport Command Britannia. Having left Tengah on 1 February, they returned there on the 8th, 'again at night'.

No 57 Sqn left for the UK on 13 August 1965. In June 1966 it was the last B 1A bomber squadron to disband and within two months Confrontation had ended. In a report on Operations in Malaysia between 1 April and 31 December 1965, C-in-C Far East (ACM Sir John Grandy) said that 'four reinforcement medium bombers (Victor or Vulcan) were retained in the Command throughout the period. This ensured that all principal targets under contingency plans were covered with forces immediately available. There is little doubt that this force has provided a valuable deterrent to Confrontation being conducted on a larger scale'. In other words, when Confrontation reached its climax in autumn 1964, the No 55 Sqn element then on station stayed beyond its allotted span. Supported by Vulcan reinforcements, the Victors helped ensure that a war of nerves never escalated out of hand, and in so doing demonstrated once again the potency and flexibility of global air power.

RECONAISSANCE AND TANKING

Given that the Victor was the longest-ranging aircraft for its time in the RAF inventory, it was always a prime candidate for the strategic reconnaissance (SR) role. A photo-reconnaissance (PR) conversion kit, capable of installation within one working week and comprising ten cameras mounted in a pre-loaded trolley, had been a feature of the Victor production specification of 1952. This tentative requirement grew to 15 cameras installed in a bomb-bay crate, together with the carriage of eight-inch photo-flashes for night PR and survey work. Prototype Victor WB775 undertook PR conversion trials, and it appeared at the 1956 Farnborough Show in the cerulean blue colours of the wartime Photographic Reconnaissance Units.

Delays in getting the Victor into service meant that the SR task was given in the first instance to Valiants allocated to No 543 Sqn at Wyton in November 1955. The Victor's reconnaissance potential was not neglected, and from March 1958 four B 1s plus crews were posted to work alongside No 543 Sqn. Led by Wg Cdr Baldwin, these Victors had no visual PR cameras but rather concentrated on radar reconnaissance, with three of them carrying a sidescan device known as Yellow Aster. The Victor Radar Reconnaissance Flight survived for a few years, but it had so little to do that it was eventually written out of existence.

Nevertheless, Handley Page continued to try and sell the reconnaissance Victor to the RAF, and during the summer of 1959, XA920 completed Radlett trials with a PR conversion pack culminating in a spectacular half loop into inverted flight to prove the systems under negative gravity. B 1 XA918 also acted as test-bed for the Red Neck sideways-looking radar attached to the underwing tank points.

All this effort was rewarded by a conference on the PR role in May 1960 which decided that a Victor be given to Boscombe Down for reconnaissance trials. XH675 took over PR development from XA920 in October 1961, and it eventually gained approval for the B 2 to take off at weights up to 223,000 lbs with full drop and bomb-bay tanks plus cameras. As all this extended the range of the reconnaissance B 2 by 40 per cent and the ceiling by

A very big Photo Shop – the Victor SR 2's camera crate sandwiched between fore and aft cylindrical long range fuel tanks. XM715 had served with Nos 139 and 100 Sqns and No 232 OCU as a B 2 prior to being converted into an SR 2, and following service with No 543 Sqn, the aircraft was modified once again into a K 2 tanker. It then spent further time with No 232 OCU, prior to seeing out its days with No 55 Sqn. Retired in November 1993, the Victor has been resident at Bruntingthorpe in private hands ever since. Maintained in operable order, XM715 made the news on 3 May 2009 when it inadvertently lifted off while undertaking a high speed taxi run

15 per cent over the PR Valiant, it was decided to re-equip No 543 Sqn with Victors. Nine aircraft were modified to a configuration known as the B(SR) 2 which allowed them to carry a cylindrical fuel tank at the front and rear of the bomb-bay with fittings in between to enable any one of four camera crate configurations to be installed for day or night reconnaissance or survey work at heights up to 50,000 ft.

The Central Reconnaissance Establishment (CRE), which became an operational group on 1 April 1963 when it assumed full responsibility for the tasking, control and training of the UK Reconnaissance Force, had been notified in March 1964 that No 543 Sqn's re-equipment with Victor SR 2s would start 'in the second quarter of 1965'. This scheduling was disturbed when fatigue cracks were found in the Valiant wing spars.

Bomber Command's six squadrons of Valiants had been expected to carry on until 1970, but on 6 August 1964, Flt Lt J W 'Taff' Foreman and his crew in Valiant WP217 were passing 30,000 ft in the climb out from Gaydon when an enormous explosion shook the whole aircraft. One of the wings sagged on landing and the crew were lucky to get down alive because a wing spar had cracked in the air. The whole Valiant force was found to be suffering from various degrees of 'crackery', and by November No 543 Sqn had been reduced to two flyable Valiants, only one of which was useable in the SR role.

The 1965 Statement on Defence did not minimise the 'difficulties in respect of in-flight refuelling and long-range photographic reconnaissance capabilities'. Fortunately, 'steps are in hand to accelerate the conversion of Victor aircraft for these roles', and the grounding of the Valiants led C-in-C Bomber Command to suggest to the Chief of Air Staff (CAS) on 12 November 1964 that the first two SR 2s should go to No 543 Sqn instead of to Boscombe Down for their trials. The RAF would thereby get the aircraft earlier and No 543 Sqn crews would benefit from flying them. CAS agreed on 27 November that No 543 Sqn should undertake equipment clearance trials, though under Ministry of Aviation direction.

All Valiants were grounded in December, and on the last day of 1964 the first No 543 Sqn crew to switch to the B 2 (Sqn Ldr John Holland (Captain), Flt Lts Roy Norman and Doug Christison (both Navigators) and Flg Off Ken Smith (AEO)) began its conversion course at No 232 OCU. After reworking, XL165 made its first flight as a SR 2 from Radlett on 23 February 1965. It was inspected at a final conference on 19 March before going to Boscombe Down for full operational assessment. No 543 Sqn's Valiants were scrapped in March, while four crews (three of them 'old hands', one a new crew) were converting to Victors at No 232 OCU.

Five No 543 Sqn Victor SR 2s and their crews stand ready for inspection at Wyton

'Dutch' Holland and his crew delivered the first new SR 2 (XL230) from Radlett to Wyton on 19 May 1965. The CRE ORB noted that further scheduled Victor deliveries between then and November would 'bring it back to operational status by the end of 1965'. At Handley Page, XM718 was undergoing repair after a heavy landing at Wittering the previous October to become the second SR 2. It was the only B 2R to be converted, albeit partially, to SR standard, and it too went to Boscombe Down before joining No 543 Sqn in January 1966.

No 543 Sqn AEO Ray Brown looks busy alongside an SR 2 camera crate while technicians remove film canisters for processing. When the Victor bomb-bay doors opened, a deflector grille dropped down to smooth the airflow. It is just visible behind the ground power cable.

The squadron's establishment of eight aircraft was achieved in April 1966, although XM716 was destroyed during a Press day at Wyton on 29 June 1966 when 'Dutch' Holland flew the big, powerful aircraft outside its limits. XM716 was overstressed in a high speed, low level turn and broke-up over the old airfield at Warboys. The Victor was a pretty forgiving aeroplane but a beast pushing out 80,000 lbs of thrust could not be treated like a Meteor. Despite the tragic loss of aircraft and crew, No 543 Sqn was back up to eight Victors again from early 1966 – just over a year after it had been withdrawn from operations.

The Victor SR 2 demonstrated its formidable range on 31 May 1966 when XL165 flew back from Piarco, Trinidad, after the Guyanan Independence celebrations. The 3896 miles to Wyton were covered in just 8 hr 21 min 20 sec without refuelling. The reconnaissance capability of the SR 2 was awesome. The camera crates inside its bomb-bay carried F96 and F49 cameras for day work and the F89 for night photography. The F96 was specially developed for high altitude use, and a fan of eight with 48-inch lenses provided excellent horizon-to-horizon cover. Four F49s were carried for survey and mapping work. For night reconnaissance, 108 photo-flashes (each of three million candlepower) were carried in three canisters, or 72 flashes in two canisters with a forward bomb-bay tank, or 36 flashes in one canister with fore and aft tanks.

The detail obtainable from the SR 2's radar is illustrated by this comparison between a post-flight radar mosaic (left) and an equivalent conventional map of the Corsican coast

The correct speed for normal Victor photography was 240-250 knots up to 40,000 ft, with the Nav Radar lining up the aircraft and opening the bomb-bay doors while the Plotter made final corrections and called 'Cameras on' from the visual aiming position. Airfields could be photographed by radar at night or in fog, with hangars, hardstandings and vehicles being pinpointed in detail. Less wholesome tasks included a survey of Saddleworth Moor during the Moors Murder case, and plotting oil spillage from the *Torrey Canyon*.

An article in the RAF magazine *Air Clues* waxed lyrical, stating that 'the Victor carries three times more photoflashes for night photography than the Valiant, and is also fitted with improved navigational equipment enabling a higher standard of accuracy to be attained. A new Rapid Processing Radar Unit is carried which provides in-flight processing of a continuous strip record of the radar picture obtained by the aircraft.

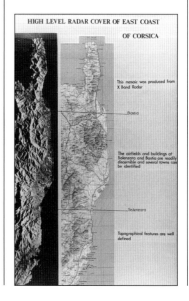

HIGH LEVEL RADAR COVER OF EAST COAST OF CORSICA

This mosaic was produced from X Band Radar

Bastia

The airfields and buildings at Solenzara and Bastia are readily discernible and several towns can be identified

Solenzara

Topographical features are well defined

'The F96 reconnaissance cameras carried in the Victor have a superior performance to the cameras carried in the Valiant and Canberra PR 7. The cameras can also be fitted with lens cones of various focal lengths, thereby providing operational flexibility. Forward coverage is three times more than before because more film can be carried in the magazines, and lateral cover on each flight-line is increased by mounting a fan of up to eight cameras so that the area covered overlaps on each camera. All the equipment is designed to provide intelligence at the largest possible scale with high resolution and minimum distortion for detailed photographic interpretation.'

A Victor could bring back 10,000 ft of exposed film to be handed over to the Wyton 'Photo Factory' for processing, and thence for interpretation at the Joint Air Reconnaissance Centre at Brampton. When all cameras were used, it was said that Kodak shares went up! No 543 Sqn also experimented with infra-red, 'false colour' and rapid processing film. However, there was never any intention that No 543 Sqn would reconnoitre the USSR, and the SR 2 carried a limited ECM fit. Visual photography was confined to 'friendly' skies and to such work as photographing ships in the North Sea or surveying Denmark in 1967.

Once it became clear that such visual work could be carried out just as well, and often more cheaply, by PR Canberras, camera crates were removed from the Victors in 1970 and radar reconnaissance came into much more prominence. Back in June 1965 HQ Bomber Command directed that, as a matter of the highest priority, 'the Victor SR 2 be assessed in the Radar Reconnaissance role to see if it is able to carry out the operational tasks previously undertaken by the Valiant (PR) Mk 1 in the maritime search role'. In September, the Wyton ORB noted that No 543 Sqn had flown three maritime cooperation exercises during the month, and that this task was becoming 'a regular and increasingly important part of the squadron's role'. The aim was 'to combine the advantage of the high, fast search capability of the Victor with the low-level capability of the long-range maritime patrol aircraft, to achieve an efficient and economical coverage of shipping movements'.

As the Soviet navy grew in strength, so the Royal Navy demanded more and more intelligence on its whereabouts. This was where No 543 Sqn excelled because one Victor could cover the whole UK in two hours, while four could survey the whole of the North Atlantic or produce a radar map of an area the size of the USA in six hours. A single SR 2 could cover an area of 400,000 square miles in eight hours, and a Nav Radar could plot every vessel in the Mediterranean on one sortie from his H2S. This allowed Defence Minister Denis Healey to make his famous statement that the British knew the position of every Soviet ship in the Mediterranean, and that they could cope with them all if the need arose.

Another Victor SR 2 survivor, XH672 of No 543 Sqn investigates a ship for itself. Although built as a B 2, this aircraft was retained as a test airframe by Handley Page and the A&AEE. Converted into an SR 2, it served with No 542 Sqn and was then converted into a K 2. After spells with Nos 57 and 55 Sqns, XH672 was retired to the Cosford Museum on 26 March 1994

A typical No 543 Sqn maritime radar reconnaissance (MRR) flight profile at 40,000 ft over the Norwegian Sea. The Nav Radar could differentiate between large, medium and small surface vessels from his radar screen and any interesting contacts were passed to a Shackleton for more detailed scrutiny at low level

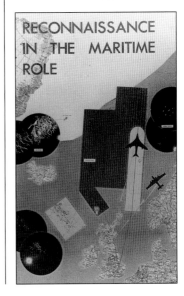

RECONNAISSANCE IN THE MARITIME ROLE

Early in 1969, No 543 Sqn's SR 2s were decked out in a new gloss polyurethane camouflage. Then in May, the unit entered two Victors in the *Daily Mail* transatlantic air race commemorating the 50th anniversary of Alcock and Brown's first direct crossing from Newfoundland to Ireland. The aim was to achieve the fastest time between the top of the GPO Tower in London and the top of the Empire State Building in New York, and XL161, aided by prevailing winds, enabled a fleet-footed co-pilot to make the eastbound journey in 5 hr 49 min 28 sec.

The final Victor SR 2 task was air sampling, known more colloquially as 'sniffing'. After atmospheric nuclear tests in the Pacific, a No 543 Sqn aircraft was detached to Peru, from where it launched to capture air samples after French nuclear tests in the South Pacific. There was also a detachment to the USAF's Shemya air base in the Alaskan Aleutian Islands to 'sniff' after a Chinese nuclear test. It was a long-range task ideally suited to the Victor, which had filter baskets containing what amounted to blotting paper placed on each drop tank nose. Meteorologists would predict the upper air flow after a nuclear test, and the Victor crew would fly through it. After landing, scientists from the Atomic Weapons Research Establishment at Aldermaston would calculate the yield of the weapon being tested from the particles on the blotting paper, and Whitehall would then know what the wily French and Chinese were up to.

SR 2 XH672 posing for a publicity photo over Norfolk in early 1969 prior to the unit's participation in the *Daily Mail* transatlantic air race

A No 543 Sqn crew back from a month-long *Pacific Ranger* to Singapore on 7 March 1969. They are, from left to right, Frank Hoare (Crew Chief), the author (Co-pilot), 'Red' Harrington (Captain), John Worrall (OC No 543 Sqn), Bas Gilbert (Nav Plotter), Geoff Rushworth (Nav Radar) and Alan Summerson (AEO). 'Zoom' Summerson had been shot down while flying a Fairey Battle over France in May 1940

AERIAL REFUELLING

If the Victor was in a good position to become a reconnaissance platform, it was a bit harder pressed to immediately assume the air refuelling role when the Valiants folded. Flight refuelling was introduced into the RAF initially for the benefit of short-range fighters. Vampires ferrying the 8618 miles to Singapore in 1953 would have had to stage through 16 airfields in

An SR 2 at Pisco, in Peru, on 29 May 1971. No 543 Sqn was detached to Jorge Chavez airport in Lima to 'sniff' French nuclear testing. Whilst here, the No 543 Sqn OC, Gordon Harper (sporting a fine moustache) decided to pay a liaison visit with the air attaché to Pisco. His co-pilot for the journey was the squadron QFI, Tom Barnard, but the two Navs and the AEO seem to have made themselves scarce (*Tom Barnard*)

B 1 XA930 with its trial fit of nose refuelling probe in late 1958. This aircraft also spent considerable time with the A&AEE and Handley Page prior to serving with Nos 10, 55 and 57 Sqns and No 232 OCU. Converted into a B(K) 1A, XA930 saw out the rest of its RAF service with Nos 214 and 55 Sqns until it was struck off charge on 17 April 1975

France, Tunis, Tripoli, Libya, Egypt, Iraq, Trucial Oman, Pakistan, India, Burma and Malaya, but as Britain withdrew from colonial possessions and found previously friendly airspace denied to it, the RAF stabilised on an eastward chain of staging posts in Malta, Cyprus, the Persian Gulf and the island of Gan, in the Indian Ocean. Thirsty fighters needed airborne refuelling to cover the intervening legs between these bases, and it was then but a short step to refuelling non-stop to do away with the en route ground servicing parties and associated support.

On 5 January 1954 the Air Staff decided that Victors and Vulcans should be capable of aerial refuelling as well. At first this was seen as 'important, not only because it will expose new targets but also because it will allow the aircraft a wider choice of routes, and so increase the task of the enemy defences'. In-flight refuelling justification then swung towards reinforcing Aden within seven hours (with one 'precautionary' flight refuelling), Gan in 11 hours (with two refuellings) and Singapore in 15 hours (with three) to reinforce the Far East. However, no V-bombers were earmarked specifically as tankers. In 1957 it was agreed that bombers would be used as necessary and 'suitably fitted as tankers when they disappear from the frontline'.

All production Victors left Radlett with a fuel system adapted for flight refuelling, and a partial trial of a refuelling probe, installed on XA921, was scheduled at Boscombe Down in 1958. This programme was delayed when XA921 was suddenly switched to conventional bombing trials, so the necessary modifications were made to XA930 instead. It first flew with probe and underwing tanks on 27 August 1958, and after appearing thus at the Farnborough airshow a week later, the aircraft was progressively modified over the next year with three different lengths of nose probe. In November 1960, after eight months of trials with a Valiant tanker, the intermediate probe length was chosen and the Victor cleared to receive fuel at 220-240 knots up to 34,000 ft, this being the maximum capability of the Valiant tanker at high weights.

The first refuelling probe was fitted to an operational B 1A when XH620 was modified by No 15 Sqn personnel in March 1962. The Victor probe stuck out like a unicorn's horn from the top of the fuselage and fuel ran to the tanks at a maximum rate of 480 gal/min via

a pipe that passed along the cockpit roof over the Nav Radar's head. No 57 Sqn B 1As were the next to be modified, but Victor B 2s came off the production line with probes attached.

Two Valiant tanker units (Nos 214 and 90 Sqns) formed, and they gave sterling service in the flight refuelling role between 1962-64, including support to eastward reinforcements by Victors and testing 'Airborne Command Post communications with Main Force V-bombers'. It was intended to generate a third Valiant unit, but on 22 November 1962 the Air Council decided that the Victor should replace the Valiant in the tanker role, and that the third tanker squadron should be formed with Victors 'as soon as possible'. The RAF hierarchy was 'satisfied that three tanker squadrons were essential to support fighter reinforcement along all the routes we might be required to use'.

The proposal to make Victor B 1/1As into tankers received endorsement early in 1963 from the Chief Scientific Adviser, MoD (Sir Solly Zuckerman), and the Chiefs of Staff. The justification was clear. The Valiant had 45,000 lbs of total transferable fuel compared with an estimated 98,500 lbs for the Victor B 1. The Valiant's maximum refuelling height and speed were 32,000 ft at Mach 0.74 compared with 40,000 ft/M 0.91 for the Victor, which was much more compatible with the frontline fighter of the time, the Lightning F 3. First generation Victors offered a longer airframe life and their only weakness was seen as 'relatively poor take-off performance'. Development cost of the Victor conversion was put at £850,000 and the estimated cost of converting 27 aircraft was £7 million.

But financial and industrial complications arose before a development contract could be placed for converting Victor B 1/1As to the tanker role. The Treasury was reluctant to agree to expenditure on a third tanker unit, or to approve the cost of modifying Victors for flight refuelling until they knew the results of the Defence Review and the deliberations of the Overseas Policy Committee on overseas commitments. The Treasury also withdrew its agreement to the modification of Victors for the first two units, even though CAS had stated these were vital to RAF operational plans. Then in August 1963 the Ministry of Aviation expressed reservations about giving a contract to Handley Page because of doubts about the company's financial soundness. However, at the end of the year the Treasury agreed in principle that 24 Victor B 1s should be converted to the tanker role. As the original estimate covering 27 aircraft for £7 million had risen, and £8 million would now convert just 24 aircraft, that is all the RAF was to be given.

Early in 1964 the second production Victor B 1, XA918, was fitted with two fuel tanks in the bomb-bay, a retractable Flight Refuelling Ltd FR 17 hose-drogue pack in the bomb-bay and two FR 20B hose-drogue pods beneath the wings. At first it was intended to make these pods interchangeable with underwing tanks on the standard strong points, but this was then found to bring the trailing drogues dangerously near the tail, so the FR 20B pods were positioned further outboard. For those of a statistical bent, the 13 ft 6 in-long Mk 20B pod was fitted 13 ft 6 in from the Victor wingtip, but no drop tanks were carried on B 1s apart from trials aircraft XA930 because the Sapphire engines were too under-powered to cope.

Servicing a Mk 20B wing pod drogue at a sunny airfield down route. To make contact, a receiver pilot simply (or frantically) flew his probe nozzle into the conical drogue while overtaking the Victor by two to five knots. As the nozzle entered, its domed nose pushed open the spring-loaded cut-off valve. The Mk 17 Hose Drogue Unit (HDU) retractable platform can be seen lowered at the back of the Victor bomb-bay

XA918 first flew as a tanker on 8 July 1964. Modifications were completed in August 1964 and the plan was to convert B 1s and B 1As to the XA918 standard as aircraft were released by the disbandment of Nos 10 and 15 Sqns. However, the complete withdrawal of Valiants from service in early 1965 made the provision of alternative tankers a matter of urgency.

On 8 February 1965, a paper was submitted to the Air Force Board proposing an interim force of six two-point Victor tankers – as opposed to the full three-point conversion – to become available from June onwards. The paper stated quite bluntly that the withdrawal of the Valiants had 'left the Royal Air Force without a flight refuelling capability', and said that under present plans for the conversion of Victors as tankers, this capability would not be restored until the first of the Victors came into service in the last quarter of 1965. With the first due to be delivered in August and to enter service in October, and an initial one-tanker-per month production rate, only five would have been produced by the end of the year, and the first squadron would not be complete until the end of February 1966.

The paper went on to say that before any flight refuelling tasks could be resumed, Victor B 1/1A bomber crews would have to be converted to the tanker role. Following this, fighter aircraft crews in both the UK and Cyprus would have to be trained in refuelling from the Victor's wing-mounted refuelling points. Six tankers were the minimum number required for this training task, and also for mounting a limited reinforcement operation. Even that limited capability would not be achieved until early 1966, and with current political tensions in the Middle East (Aden) and Far East (Confrontation), such an operational limitation was unacceptable. It was therefore essential to get six tanker aircraft into service 'as rapidly as possible'.

Three alternative ways of achieving this were considered in the paper – borrowing or buying USAF tankers, speeding-up the existing Victor three-point tanker conversion programme or fast-tracking six partially modified Victor tankers. The first two were rejected. If there were a loan or purchase of American aircraft, air- and groundcrews to operate them 'would hardly have completed training before re-training on the Victors became necessary'. As to the second course, converting a Victor to a three-point refueller – two points in wing-mounted pods for fighters and one in the fuselage for bombers and transport aircraft – took eight/nine months. Acceleration of the first six three-point tankers was not possible because there was insufficient time to advance the delivery of the long-dated materials required for the modification kits and some sub-contracted equipment.

The third alternative – producing six partially modified Victors – could be achieved either by fitting only the central fuselage refuelling point, or by fitting only the wing pod installations. The supply of components for the latter was further ahead than for the former, and wing pods presented a simpler modification and permitted a much quicker turn-round time. The fact that wing pod installations would not be able to refuel V-bomber aircraft was deemed 'acceptable' since this was 'not vital to current reinforcement plans'.

A Handley Page study showed that six aircraft could be produced by the end of August 1965, deliveries starting with two in June. Clearance flying could be completed on the prototype tanker which was already flying. As Victors already converted by the company were 'in an advanced state of strip-down and re-build', it was proposed to feed six fully serviceable B 1As into a special conversion line and to embody 'only those modifications essential to give them the two-point refuelling capability'.

Standard bomber-type overload fuel tanks would be carried in the bomb-bay, giving a total of 81,000 1bs of fuel, of which 48,000 1bs could be transferred through the wing-mounted installations. This would give 'a similar capability to that of the Valiant tanker, with the added advantage of two refuelling points'. The proposed crash programme to produce six two-point Victor tankers was expected to incur an extra cost of about £0.5 million, assuming that they would eventually be brought up to the full tanker specification. The first of the six B 1As had to be fed into the conversion line early in February and the last early in March. Under the existing timetable for Victor squadron run-downs, it would be possible to provide aircraft to meet this programme without affecting the planned V-force frontline strength.

On 8 February 1965 the go-ahead was given for the conversion to proceed immediately. Three days later, the Vice Chief of Air Staff told the Defence Minister that Handley Page had said they could produce six two-point tankers by the end of August 1965, the first two being delivered in June. In fact Handley Page managed to get the first two Victor two-point tankers to the RAF by May, even though the company's Radlett factory was concurrently busy with the conversion of the nine Victor SR 2s for No 543 Sqn.

As B 1As returned from Cottesmore after disbandment of Nos 10 and 15 Sqns, six were converted into two-point tankers using the wing-mounted FR 20B hose-drogue pods already under trial on XA918. A fully loaded FR 20B pod weighed 2000 lbs, and it included a two-bladed ram air turbine to provide hydraulic and fuel pressure via a gearbox, a 145-gal fuel tank replenished from the aircraft's fuel system and a hose drum unit around which was wound a 51-ft hose with a 1½-inch internal bore. The end of the hose was connected to the Mk VIII drogue coupling to enable fuel to be passed to a receiver up to a rate of 1200 lb/min. Coloured lights to act as 'traffic indicators' were fitted to each pod so that refuelling could be carried out in radio silence, and the only other addition to the aircraft was a second bomb-bay tank to give a total transferable fuel load of 48,000 lbs.

These six interim tankers, which still retained their bombing capability, were designated B(K) 1As, and Radlett laboured round the clock to such effect that the first, XH620, was flying on 28 April 1965. 'Spud' Murphy was test pilot on the Victor tanker project because he had previous experience at Vickers with Valiant tankers. He received a Queen's

A receiver's eye view of the bomb-bay mounted Mk 17 HDU

Commendation for bringing the two-point tanker in 17 weeks early.

Priority Boscombe Down handling trials with Lightning and Sea Vixen contacts were concluded by 21 May, during which the presence of a Mk 20B pod under each wing was found to make no significant changes to the Victor's flying characteristics. The B(K) 1A was pleasant to fly, and Boscombe Down cleared it for a maximum take-off weight of 185,000 lbs and a top speed of 330 knots/Mach 0.93.

No 55 Sqn, which was to operate the two-point tankers, became non-operational as a Medium Bomber Force squadron at Honington on 1 March 1965 and moved to Marham on 24 May to begin its new task. The first two B(K) 1A aircraft (XH602 and XH648) arrived at Marham on 25 May, and by month end No 55 Sqn had received two more (XH667 and XH620). By June the squadron strength was up to five aircraft, and the Minister for the RAF (Lord Shackleton) informed the Minister of Aviation (Roy Jenkins) on 3 June that the Air Force Board had expressed 'great appreciation' at the way the company had 'helped us over a rather critical situation in regard to tankers following the grounding of the Valiants'.

No 55 Sqn crews were sufficiently up to speed in their new tanking role to ferry four Lightnings of No 74 Sqn out from Wattisham to Akrotiri on 14 August. All arrived on schedule after an average flight time of 4 hr 10 min, marking the first occasion that the Victor tanker had been used for an operational overseas deployment. Four No 19 Sqn Lightnings were ferried back to Leconfield, although a one-day delay was incurred by a double pod failure. No 19 Sqn pilots found no undue difficulty in converting to the Victor from the Valiant, the unit also investigating low-level tanking, which they found to be an interesting experience. 'Flt Lts Scott and Wratten, the pilots involved, have found that this sort of display flying is possible only if the "plug-in" is carried out over the sea – where conditions are relatively smooth. The Victor's wing is particularly prone to flexing in turbulence, and the whip effect at the basket end of the drogue is quite frightening if a Lightning is not on the end to tone it down.'

Flight magazine reported on 19 August that 'the first Victor tankers have two refuelling points – the hoses and drogues are unwound from two underwing pods which can be used simultaneously. When the "customer" has made contact, he edges forward until the yellow part of the hose has wound back to the pod and he is then in the optimum position for accepting fuel, which starts to flow automatically. The Victor captain flies the tanker while the co-pilot manages the 31-cell fuel system and keeps a check on tanker cg (centre of gravity) movements. The navigator/radar works the pod and hose-trailing controls. Most fuel transfers are performed in stable air above 30,000 ft. It takes about four minutes to refuel a fighter and about ten minutes for a bomber. The Victor B 1A tanker conversion carries 52,850 1bs of transferable fuel.

'The present two-point tankers will not be converted to the three-point standard to which later Victor conversions will be made.

'The three-point refueller will have an additional hose/drogue unit on the fuselage underside. This will be a tremendous advance on the old single-point Valiant tanker on which failure of the hose/drogue equipment meant the complete waste of the sortie. The RAF will subsequently form two more Victor tanker squadrons at Marham.'

By October No 55 Sqn had its full strength of six B(K) 1As, and that month it went further afield to Tehran, refuelling four Lightning F 3s of No 74 Sqn which were to participate in an Imperial Iranian Air Force Day. Exercise *Donovan* involved supporting the Lightnings from Akrotiri to Iran and on their return flight. During its first 18 months in service, No 55 Sqn took part in 39 overseas exercises and transferred 6,718,700 lbs of fuel from its 12 drogues during 3143 wet contacts.

On 2 November 1965 the first three-point Victor tanker conversion, XA937, took to the air. The ten Victors initially modified to this configuration were selected from the original B 1 production batch and were in consequence eventually known as Victor K 1s. Although externally similar to the B(K) 1A, the K 1s were very different internally. They carried Mk 20B wing pods and a nose probe, but most significantly they lost their bombing capability when their bomb-bay doors were removed and two 15,300-lb fuel tanks and a Mk 17 Hose Drum Unit (HDU) were fitted in their bomb-bays.

The Mk 17 HDU was mounted on a retractable platform so that the scoop containing the hose and drogue could be lowered by a jack connected to the old bomb-bay door hydraulics. The HDU initially carried a 93-ft hose with a three-inch internal bore, but this was soon found to snake violently when disturbed by unstable air, much to the amusement (or horror) of receiver pilots who were then treated to the interesting sight of a hose that fluctuated from the near vertical to the horizontal. After Boscombe Down trials, the problem was solved by shortening the hose to 80 ft and fitting a modified drogue.

No 57 Sqn followed No 55 Sqn over to Marham in December 1965. Four Victors flew in formation over Marham on 1 December 1965 to signal the unit's arrival, whereupon one of them, XA930, was delivered to Radlett for modification as a three-point tanker. The first three-point tanker, XA937, arrived back at Marham on 14 February 1966 but it was not available for flying until March. Aircrews concentrated on continuation training in their existing Victors, and initiated a trials programme to confirm performance data for the three-point tanker and to establish a Tacan/Collins rendezvous procedure. Lightnings took the opportunity to 'prod' on familiarisation and handling sorties.

No 57 Sqn became operational in the tanker role on 1 June 1966, by which time eight of its crews had achieved the classification Operational (Tanking) and it had six K 1 aircraft modified for the role. No 57 Sqn completed its first operational tanking exercise, with Lightnings to and from Cyprus, in conjunction with three crews from No 55 Sqn. The last day of June saw No 57 Sqn 'with one crew at Akrotiri and two at Wheelus AFB (Tripoli, Libya), having by now completed five Exercise *Forthright 46/47* sorties with all rendezvous and transfers completed as planned'. The HDUs were generally reserved for large aircraft, and in October 1966, No 57 Sqn successfully proved the ventral arrangement in trials with a VC10 shortly after the strategic transport entered service with the original Victor unit, No 10 Sqn.

A Victor K 1 could carry enough fuel to keep a Lightning airborne for 17 hours, and tanker support thereby considerably extended the air defender's range, flexibility and effectiveness. Dotted around the coast of Britain were six 'towlines' to which fighters would be directed by their air defence radar controllers. The Victor Nav Radar, who monitored the refuelling exercise, could watch thirsty contacts approach by using the Fishpool mode on his H2S radar. As they closed, he could trail the winghoses in 20 seconds, before passing sustaining fuel.

On very long overseas flights, two Victors would fly in company with the fighters, each refuelling a 'chick' about every 30 minutes. As the Victors were themselves depleted, one tanker would top up the other via the HDU before returning to base. The second Victor would continue with the fighters, replenishing as required, until it too was replaced by a new pair of tankers. This process was repeated down the route.

As B 1A bombers returned to Radlett, 14 were converted to three-point tankers known eventually as K 1As. With two Victor tanker squadrons now in business, a third was formed in August 1966 to bring the flight refuelling force up to its planned strength. No 214 Sqn, which had been the original Valiant tanker unit, was officially re-formed at Marham on 1 July with an establishment of eight B(K) 1/1As, although it was not until 1 August that the first two crews, including the CO, Wg Cdr D Mullarkey, finished their Tanker Training Flight courses. Three more crews were posted in from No 57 Sqn on 8 August, and initially No 214 Sqn borrowed aircraft from No 57 Sqn, but the first of its own Victor tankers (XA938) was delivered to Marham on 27 September.

By the end of 1966 No 214 Sqn had seven K 1/1As out of an establishment of eight, and in February 1967 – in what its ORB described as 'the most eventful month so far for the squadron' – it had four crews involved in Exercise *Forthright 59/60*, taking Lightning F 3s to Akrotiri and returning with F 6s, which meant that it was by now fully operational as part of the tanker force. Around that time No 55

A Victor K 1 simultaneously refuels two Phantom FGR 2s that are themselves carrying external tanks. The Victor tanker could land with a hose extended, although it could also be jettisoned in an emergency provided the hose was fully trailed

Sqn, which had initiated the Victor flight-refuelling role with the interim two-point tankers, started re-equipping with the three-point version.

By February 1967, No 55 Sqn had two two-point and three three-point tankers, against an establishment for five two-point K 1s and three three-point K 1As. At the same time, No 55 Sqn relinquished its tanker conversion responsibilities to the Tanker Training Flight (TTF), which took over three of the two-point tankers while the remaining trio were distributed around the units as 'hacks'. They were known henceforward as B 1A (K 2P)s. In 1970, the TTF was redesignated No 232 OCU.

The three-squadron Victor tanker force at Marham was operational from early 1967 to the extent that in June, it successfully flight-refuelled 13 Lightning F 6s of No 74 Sqn from Leuchars to Tengah, Singapore, and back in Operation *Hydraulic*. When on 12 June 1967, Wg Cdr P B McCorkindale, O C No 55 Sqn since 25 May 1965, handed over command to Wg Cdr R A Harvey, it was recorded in the ORB that 'much of the credit for speedily converting the Victor into an operational tanker after the demise of the Valiant must go to him'.

By the time the last conversion was completed in June 1967, Handley Page had produced six two-point and 24 three-point tankers. In June 1968, a Hastings and Victor K 1 XA927 from No 57 Sqn represented all the aircraft ever built by Handley Page in the Queen's Review static display at Abingdon. Overhead six B 2Rs from Wittering led a 24-ship flypast, but it was to be the swansong of the Victor bomber because from now on the Handley Page tradition lay solely with the tanker.

FATIGUE

Every day from 1963, two Victor B 2Rs – one from each of Nos 100 and 139 Sqns – had sat on the Wittering ORP with their crews on QRA. Two-dozen practice alerts, codenamed 'EDOM', might be called in an average month, half of them being up to engine start and nearly one-quarter involving taxiing to the take-off position. But whereas the Vulcan continued in service after Royal Navy Polaris submarines took over strategic deterrent responsibility, metal fatigue killed off the Victor bomber as surely as it did the Valiant.

Assuming an effective fatigue life of more than 5000 flying hours, and that crews were allowed 32 hours' low-level training a year, back in 1963 it was estimated that the V-force would not become life-expired until about 1970. However, no-one foresaw the Valiant fatigue problem which centred on aircraft structures as well as flying hours.

In their quest for better performance after 1945, aircraft designers became so weight-conscious that they rejected the old wartime light aluminium alloys in favour of new high strength, light zinc-bearing forged alloys known as DTD 683 and DTD 687. These double heat-treated plates were extremely strong as well as light, but their long-term properties were unknown, and it was eventually found that they became brittle, with a high propensity to stress fatigue. Anodising had no effect but lanoline prolonged fatigue life, so it was used in the manufacture of the Victor just as it had coated Frederick Handley Page's 'Yellow Peril' monoplane in 1912.

Yet in fairness to all concerned, when the Victors were built there was not the range of alternatives there is today. 'Because they were high strength alloys', said Ken Pratt, who ran the Handley Page Test House and experimental workshop, 'they were the only things you would use in big structure members and skins that enabled you to get the structural weight to something half decent. If we had known then what we know now about DTD 683 (used in forgings and extrusions), we would not have used it, but if we hadn't used 683 the aircraft would have been much heavier, or we would have had a gap of seven ot ten years before alternatives became available to build an aeroplane that did as well as the Victor did'.

Because a bomber did not have as long an operational life as a transport in terms of flying hours, the specialists believed that there were adequate safeguards against stress cracking and premature fatigue failure. 'We had a tremendously redundant structure', said Godfrey Lee, 'with distributed flanges and a multitude of bolts holding the wings together, unlike the Valiant which was dependent on a few spars'. A complete change in role altered the situation. The Victor was designed to spend the majority of its operational life in the calm upper air, encountering turbulence simply in the climb and descent, but from 1963 the aircraft found themselves in a completely new low-level flight regime. Handley Page considered reducing wing span, but it is very difficult to reduce span on a swept-wing aircraft without generating a host of new problems, and anyway a complete rebuild would have been necessary to strengthen the structure.

Unfortunately, whereas the massive strength of the Vulcan wing, plus reinforcement in anticipation of Skybolt, would sustain the delta at low level into the 1980s, the Victor had a more flexible wing. The Victor was more comfortable to fly at low level because it rode out the gusts and turbulence as the wings flexed up and down like giant shock absorbers. 'We used to practice one manoeuvre', recalled a No 139 Sqn captain, which simulated the failure of the Blue Steel motor. We would rush in at 350 knots, pull up at 1.5g to 11,000 ft and then release the missile on the Nav Radar's call like a free-fall bomb. This was all very well, but whenever we pulled up from low level, you could hear the wings crack'.

Thus by the time Nos 100 and 139 Sqns disbanded in 1968, the lower boom forgings which provided the mainplane attachments were cracked on most B 2Rs. All but two aircraft were flown down from Wittering to Radlett to be mothballed.

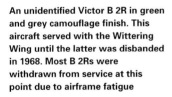

An unidentified Victor B 2R in green and grey camouflage finish. This aircraft served with the Wittering Wing until the latter was disbanded in 1968. Most B 2Rs were withdrawn from service at this point due to airframe fatigue

VICTOR TRIUMPHANT – FALKLANDS TO IRAQ

Marham tankers helped a Royal Navy Phantom FG 1 clock-up the fastest time of all during the 1969 *Daily* Mail transatlantic air race, and there were to be many other demonstrations of the value of what was now termed air-to-air refuelling (AAR). During the 1974 Cyprus emergency, for example, the commander of the United Nations' peace-keeping force made an urgent request for RAF support. Taking-off at two hours notice from Britain on the night of 24 July, 12 Phantom FGR 2s were on ten minutes standby in Akrotiri by first light on 25 July thanks to Victor assistance.

Although K 1 and K 1A Victors could transfer their own weight in fuel, their performance was restricted by their Sapphire engines. More powerful B 2Rs made redundant by the disbandment of the Wittering Wing were natural successors because they could add two drop tanks worth of fuel to every towline and would be less limited when operating out of hot-and-high airfields.

The K 2 conversion contract was technically agreed with Handley Page in October 1969, but it was initially limited to design and feasibility studies, much to Radlett's financial chagrin. In an effort to maintain its independence after Sir Frederick's death, Handley Page decided in August 1965 to concentrate on a short-haul turboprop passenger transport called the HP 137 Jetstream. Orders were not slow in coming, particularly from across the Atlantic, but the prototype and early production aircraft were overweight, and by the end of 1968 the company had spent £5.5 million on development. This drain on finances was not eased by a slump in the aviation market. Buyers held back from parting with ready cash until the Jetstream reached its brochure performance, and the only

XL232 is seen with all of its hoses trailing. This aircraft spent time with Nos 139 and 100 Sqns, No 232 OCU and the Wittering Wing prior to becoming to the first Victor B 2 to fly after conversion into a K 2 by Hawker Siddeley. It subsequently served with No 55 Sqn on four occasions, No 232 OCU again and No 57 Sqn twice. The aircraft was consumed by fire after an engine failed shortly after its brakes were released for take-off at Marham on 15 October 1982 (see photograph on page 89)

quick way of achieving this was to install more powerful engines, which demanded more money and time.

'We felt sure', said Godfrey Lee, 'that we who had done the Victor could quickly do a small 300 mph twin turboprop aeroplane. I think we all underestimated the difficulties of the task we had undertaken'. By the time full certification was in sight in August 1969, the Jetstream development bill had topped £13 million, representing a break-even requirement of 1000 sales instead of the original 400. Creditors started asking for cash instead of extending credit, and for a company with all its money tied up on the shop floor, the only solution was to go into voluntary liquidation on 8 August. A rescue operation was mounted with American money, but it was very dependent on the Victor K 2 conversion contract being confirmed. 'We could have survived with £1.5 million from the Ministry of Defence', said Reggie Stafford, but the tanker lifeline was never thrown and on 2 March 1970 employees arriving at Radlett were sent home, apart from a skeleton staff to provide product support for RAF Victors.

Within two months, the K 2 contract was awarded to Hawker Siddeley, and between April and July the 21 Victors mothballed at Radlett, plus the veteran trials B 1 XA922, were transferred to the old Avro factory at Woodford that had sired the Vulcan. Sir Frederick Handley Page must have turned in his grave.

The prototype K 2, XL231, first flew from Woodford on 1 March 1972, but it did not have its internal structure completely updated. Still in its Wittering colours, XL231 was destined initially for Boscombe Down, where close circuit TV was installed to monitor the behaviour of refuelling equipment in flight. Only later was it reworked to the full K 2 production standard.

The conversion contract specifically stated that there was to be no reversionary bomber role, so out went all the Blue Steel and free-fall weapons equipment, the Window and ECM fit, apart from the Blue Saga passive warning receiver, and all electrical cable looms and other accessories that were superfluous to in-flight refuelling. Few external changes were immediately apparent. The most obvious was the Mk 17 HDU in the bomb-bay plus underwing Mk 20B refuelling pods alongside the existing drop tanks – the latter were no longer jettisonable, however. A keener eye would have detected a new tail cone, incorporating

Victor K 1 XA937 (captained by Jim Uprichard) refuels K 1 XA932 (captained by Alan Mawby). This photograph, taken from an accompanying Harrier GR 1 on 2 May 1972, shows the higher nose attitude of the receiver aircraft due to the downwash behind the tanker. After almost two decades of frontline service, both of these Victors were retired in early February 1977 (*Alan Mawby*)

The undersides of a K 2 tanker and its Phantom FGR 2 receiver in August 1977. The underside of a Victor tanker was painted white with Dayglo orange markings to help a receiver pilot line up properly for contact with the drogue

a fuel jettison facility, and one-and-a-half feet were taken off each wingtip (making a total span of 117 ft) to reduce wing fatigue. Handley Page had intended to add small 350-gal capacity tip tanks to act as bob weights, but despite funding completion of this design study, Hawker Siddeley finally opted for the alternative method of decreasing wing loads by reducing span to move the centre of pressure inboard.

Structural refurbishment inside the wing also concentrated on known fatigue areas, especially around the mainplane attachment, to restore the airframe fatigue index to zero. Zinc-free DTD 5104 was used on the forgings in place of DTD 683, and L73 in lieu of DTD 687 for the skins.

XL233 was the first Victor K 2 tanker to reach the frontline, and it is seen here shortly after arriving at Marham from Woodford on 8 May 1974. The tanker is already wearing the crest of No 232 OCU on its tail. XL233 was retired by No 55 Sqn on 25 September 1988 (*Mawby*)

Another early K 2 conversion, this ex-B 2R in green and grey camouflage carries the No 232 OCU marking on its fin. The tanker is seen landing at Marham following a training flight in the late 1970s

Riveting replaced spot-welding in the new sandwich skin parts and the gauge of the skins and corrugations was increased. Each K 2 emerged from Woodford with a design life of 14 years free from fatigue problems.

Inside the cockpit the fuel control panel was completely redesigned to cope with 127,000 lbs of fuel, and the pilots' flying instrumentation panels were updated and finished in a chic shade of grey. Among rear cabin improvements was the installation of a new Smiths Industries' rear view periscope incorporating a swivelling eyepiece to see all customers.

The first production K 2 to enter service, XL233, joined No 232 OCU at Marham on 8 May 1974. Normal maximum take-off weight was 223,000 lbs, but when operationally essential, weight could be increased to 238,000 lbs. There was a proposal to resurrect rocket-assisted take-off for such heavy loads, but nothing came of this, although it was recognised that overweight operations would reduce the structural strength reserve.

Twenty-eight B 2s were initially earmarked for conversion to K 2s, beginning with the 21 B 2Rs. The remainder were to have come from No 543 Sqn, which duly disbanded on 31 May 1974 when its radar reconnaissance role was taken over by No 27 Sqn Vulcan B 2MRRs. An SR 2 flight of four aircraft was kept in being at Wyton until 30 May 1975 to monitor French nuclear tests in the Pacific, but in the end this made no difference because financial constraints eventually allowed only 24 Victors to be modified to K 2s. As this number was regarded as only sufficient to re-equip Nos 55 and 57 Sqns, plus No 232 OCU, the doyen of flight refuellers, No 214 Sqn, had to be disbanded on 28 January 1977

Keeping it in the family, Pete Ferguson, Flight Commander Training on No 232 OCU, captains this No 55 Sqn K 2 during refuelling trials at 20,000 ft in January 1978 with Tornado IDS prototype 03, flown by his younger brother Tim, who was Deputy Chief Test Pilot at Warton

when its K 1s and K 1As were phased out.

From now on the Marham Wing stabilised into an almost daily routine of supporting the RAF fighter force in its defence of UK airspace. For air defence Lightnings and Phantom FGR 2s flying hundreds of miles offshore, loiter time was of major importance and their hard points were better used for weapons than drop tanks. Once it was appreciated that time on station could be tripled without affecting crew fatigue, Victor tankers became a valued 'force multiplier'.

A No 57 Sqn line-up of K 2s at Marham in the early 1980s. Note their near uniformity in camouflage and markings

So might the Victor force have remained largely outside the public eye had it not been for the Argentinean invasion of the Falkland Islands on 2 April 1982. It was clear from the start of Operation *Corporate* that the Victor tanker fleet would have an important role to play in any attempt to reassert British sovereignty. Yet despite manpower support from No 232 OCU, there were fewer than two dozen Victor K 2s available to supplement South Atlantic operations, and the air defence of the UK could not be neglected. So even those crews recently arrived at Marham had to be capable of carrying out the most demanding aspect of their craft – mid-air refuelling of the tankers themselves by day or night. The latest navigation equipment was also installed for very long flights over water, together with an improvised camera fit in some K 2 noses.

By 18 April, Nos 55 and 57 Sqns were in a position to detach six Victors to Wideawake, the mid-Atlantic staging airfield on Ascension Island. Some 2850 miles away lay South Georgia, the first objective to be recovered from Argentina. Before a landing could take place, however, the British had to know whether the Argentinean Navy was in the area in strength. With the reconnaissance Vulcans of No 27 Sqn having been retired just a month previously, Victor tankers were the only aircraft immediately available, and suitable, for carrying out maritime radar reconnaissance over the vast distances involved.

At 0250 hrs local time on 20 April 1982, the first of four tankers, all at the maximum take-off all up weight of 223,000 lbs, took off from Wideawake, followed by the others at one minute intervals. Each Victor carried an additional crew member, a specialist Nav Rad in the Maritime Radar Reconnaissance (MRR) role borrowed from the Vulcan Force. It was at the top of the climb out when each aircraft checked its centre hose that XL192's was found to be unserviceable. The only thing for an aircraft that could not give away fuel was to take over the primary role. It was then that the No 55 Sqn crew – Sqn Ldr John Elliott, Flg Off Dick Evans, Sqn Ldr Al Beedie, Sqn Ldr Mike Buxey, Flt Lt Ray Chapple and the additional MRR specialist, Sqn Ldr Tony Cowling – moved from a supporting role into the lead role to radar reconnoitre an area to the north of South Georgia.

At about 1000 miles south of Ascension, two Victors gave all their spare fuel to the other pair and then returned to base. For the two

A Victor K 2 refuels a Nimrod MR 2P maritime patrol aircraft in April 1982 as part of an urgent trial to extend the latter aircraft's range during the Falklands campaign

receivers, it was their first night on-load to the in-flight maximum all-up-weight of 238,000 lbs. Two hours and 1000 miles later, another transfer of fuel took place, and then John Elliott and his crew were on their own.

Arriving off the northeast tip of South Georgia at dawn, XL192 descended from 43,000 ft to 18,000 ft so that Tony Cowling could scan all around for contacts on his H2S. The search took just over 90 minutes and covered an area of more than 150,000 square miles – the equivalent of the whole of the British Isles – before the Victor returned to Ascension late in the afternoon courtesy of another four tankers. Having been airborne for 14 hr 45 min and covered about 6500 nautical miles, the Elliott crew brought back radar information to show that there were no warships of any size in the area, and that the northern approaches were iceberg free. In so doing, both they and XL192 captured the record for the longest-ranging operational reconnaissance mission to date.

Two further air refuelled Victor maritime radar reconnaissance missions were flown before this task was handed over to RAF Nimrods with their more advanced sensors. The delay in employing these specialist aircraft was caused by the need to modify Nimrods, and train their crews, so that they too could refuel in the air. Two 'fill-ups' were required on each outbound Nimrod leg from Ascension, and one more during the return. This alone did not account for the number of support Victors required, but rather it was always necessary, over such great distances, to refuel the refuellers. Thus when the first Vulcan bombing mission was mounted against Port Stanley airfield early in the morning of 1 May, this single operation called for no fewer than 11 Victor support sorties outbound and a further five at the rendezvous (RV) point on the return.

The RAF had not flown such a coordinated, big aircraft operation since World War 2, and even then no Bomber Command raid had equated to a flight from England to bomb Chicago airport and return. More than 80 aircrew gathered for the pre-flight briefing in a flapping tent at Wideawake for what was basically to be a Victor operation, launching a stand-off Vulcan at the very end.

A primary and a reserve Vulcan took off on the operation, codenamed 'Black Buck 1'. In the event, the primary aircraft would not pressurise in the climb so the secondary crew took over the mantle. Ahead of them, at one minute intervals, had roared off 11 Victor tankers, of which two were reserves – one was needed because a Victor crew found that they could not wind out their HDU, but the second returned to base.

In the van of the 'Black Buck' formation was the 'tanker lead', who was always an experienced Victor captain. The first fuel transfer, supervised by tanker leader Sqn Ldr Mike Todd, took place about one-and-three-quarter hours after take-off some 840 miles south of Ascension. Four Victors topped up the tanks of four others and then turned back. This 'cascade' system was repeated a number of times thereafter until only one Victor remained with the bomber.

Unfortunately, after five-and-a-half hours in the air, events 2750 miles south of Ascension were not going to plan. For a start, the Vulcan's fuel consumption was considerably greater than forecast because it was operating at higher than normal weights and the recently fitted underwing ECM pod was causing extra drag. In addition, because the heavy Victors could not reach the optimum Vulcan operating height, the bomber had to keep descending to a less economical level to refuel.

To cap it all, after topping up the Vulcan's tanks once more, Sqn Ldr Bob Tuxford in XL189 found that he had to refuel the remaining Victor right over the top of violent storm clouds. Flt Lt Steve Biglands' Victor (XH669) closed in behind Tuxford's, only to see the hose and basket dancing up and down by about 20 ft. After some superb flying, Biglands managed to get his probe into the drogue, but it broke before the transfer was complete. There was nothing for it but for Tuxford and Biglands to change places, and for Tuxford to take back the fuel he had just given away plus sufficient for the Vulcan to reach Port Stanley. The skies cleared to make this possible, but the airborne minuet had taken the penultimate Victor well south of where it should have turned back. XH669 therefore not only had to fly further to get home, but Biglands also had to retain a reasonable reserve because his broken probe prevented him from taking on any more fuel.

When the Vulcan refuelled for the last time before descending towards its target just over an hour away, it was still some 6000 lbs short when

Mission over, a No 55 Sqn K 2 lands back at Ascension Island during the Falklands War. Of the RAF's 23-strong Victor K 2 fleet, only three aircraft did not operate from Ascension Island during hostilities. One was undergoing routine maintenance and two were fully committed to flying training missions or supporting deployments from Marham

XL190, with a locally modified paint scheme, was photographed at Marham just after returning from Ascension Island. The nosewheel door is missing because the aircraft was undergoing repairs at the time following failure of the nosewheel to lower on landing (*Millard*)

XH669 of No 57 Sqn returned to Marham with Strategic Air Command striping after being zapped during a visit to a US Air National Guard base whilst supporting RAF assets on exercise in North America (*Millard*)

Tuxford flashed his red lights to indicate that the transfer was over. He had sacrificed so much before peeling away and heading north that he would need a tank-up himself if XL189 was not to ditch 400 miles south of Ascension.

The second part of the mission was to get all the aircraft safely back to Wideawake. The first four Victors to return were so short of fuel that they had to land in stream, thereby putting all that good short landing practise with the brake 'chute to good use. For the Tuxford crew it was a longer, drier journey home. 'We discussed a lot of things, including the practical aspects of bailing out of a Victor into the sea – you could not hope to ditch it for the aircraft is the wrong shape. We had our radar on to see it there were any ships in the area, but in fact there was none in the right place'.

Fortunately Tuxford was able to rendezvous with one of the first wave tankers that had been hurriedly turned round and sent to meet him, while an equally apprehensive Vulcan crew arrived at their first tanking point off the coast of Brazil critically short of fuel. They need not have worried because, exactly to plan, the white underside of another of the first wave Victors swung into position. It was, in the words of the Vulcan captain, 'the most beautiful sight in the world'. For his selfless efforts, Bob Tuxford was awarded the AFC.

With the first Vulcan raid judged to be a success, 'Black Buck 2' was launched late in the evening of 3 May. The lessons of two days earlier had been taken to heart, and instead of one huge formation going south, shedding tankers like leaves off a tree, 'Black Buck 2' consisted of two smaller groups. The first contained the Vulcan and its immediate replenishers, who took the bomber two-thirds of the way to Port Stanley before the last Victor turned back. The second tanker wave took off about five minutes after the first, and they flew at a slightly greater height and speed so that they caught up well down the route. Their eventual task

was to fill a single Victor full of fuel so that it could replenish the Vulcan immediately prior to its descent towards the target. In the words of the captain of the Vulcan concerned, the tanker plan 'worked like magic – people were throwing fuel at us from every direction'.

Victors would escort a Vulcan down to Port Stanley on four more occasions, and only one of these missions had to be aborted when, just before the penultimate 'prod', two Victors were unable to pass fuel to each other because of a failure in the donor's HDU. By the last Vulcan raid on 12 June, Victor crews had refined their performance to such an extent that the bomber captain described the sortie as 'almost old hat'.

But Victors and their crews were 'extending' other types besides the Vulcan. Nimrods searched the sea for diesel submarines, crucial Harrier replacements were flown out to reinforce the invading Task Force and Hercules transports eventually dropped high-priority supplies over a free, but unusable, Port Stanley airfield, all courtesy of the ubiquitous Victor.

The scale of air-refuelling operations from Ascension Island during *Corporate* was such that tanker aircrews were regularly flying up to 120 hours a month, much of it at night or in unpredictable weather conditions. Peacetime aircraft flying rates were trebled and, frequently, 15 out of the 16 Victors at Wideawake were needed to meet the daily tasking. Over a two-month period these tankers flew some 3000 hrs on 530 combat missions, giving away 23 million pounds weight of fuel in the process. During the whole South Atlantic campaign, only three missions failed through malfunction of the Victor's refuelling equipment, and none had to be cancelled as a result of tanker aircraft unserviceability. It was a remarkable record, and in the words of AVM Michael Knight, AOC No 1 Group, in which the tankers now served, 'the outstanding performance of the ageing Victor and its crews was the very cornerstone of air operations in support of the Falklands Task Force'.

Victors continued to be heavily committed in the South Atlantic even when hostilities ended. Their task eased with the introduction of the Hercules tanker and the reopening of Port Stanley airfield, but it only ended on 10 June 1985 when the newly opened Mount Pleasant airfield was in a position to receive wide body jets.

Meanwhile, back at Woodford, the old Radlett B 2 fatigue specimen, consisting of a fuselage and mainplanes, was continuing the good work as the K 2 specimen. Unfortunately, in November 1982 it revealed the old Wittering problem of serious cracks in both the port and starboard wing lower booms. The bottom boom was the most critical part of the wing structure, being in torsion during flight, and by the time the cracks were found, propagation was too extensive to be arrested by repair. Major refurbishment was also discounted because it was more cost-effective to convert ex-civil airline VC10s and TriStars to the tanker role. The fuel transfer capacity of a TriStar being equal to that of eight Victors, it was decided to set a maximum Victor fatigue life limit based on that of the specimen airframe and leave it at that.

Ironically, while Victor Conway engine problems dramatically reduced during the Falklands campaign, perhaps demonstrating the benefit of using machinery constantly, the high intensity of heavily-laden South Atlantic operations had taken its toll of Victor airframe life. 'Young' K 2s, such as XL164 with only 1626 hours on the clock from new, were

A Victor flies off into the sunset during the twilight of the aircraft's career

When a fully laden Victor tanker caught fire, it burned ferociously. This was all that remained of XL232 after its No 3 engine exploded as the brakes were released for take-off on 15 October 1982. Fortunately, all crew members escaped without injury

a rarity, and some of the others were rapidly ageing. The force was also being eroded by accidents such as that to XL232, which was destroyed on 15 October 1982 following failure of a turbine disc.

Consequently it was decided to retire the least sustainable aircraft and disband No 232 OCU in April 1986, together with No 57 Sqn on 30 June. This left an enlarged No55 Sqn with ten aircraft, plus five in-use reserves. The unit switched to four-man crew operations during 1986 by the simple expedient of re-positioning the AAR controls to the AEO's left side and removing one navigator's seat and mounting the other seat on rails so that it could slide sideways to cover both navigating stations. The remaining navigator, who probably felt he deserved double pay even though some of the Nav Radar's kit had been deleted, must have been comforted by the Boscombe Down reassurance that 'no safety or operational problems are encountered by aircrew within the 3rd and 99th percentile anthropometric range'!

The plan was for the each remaining Victor to retire as it reached its limiting fatigue life. Then on 8 August 1990, while supporting RAF Jaguars deployed to a Reconnaissance Air Meet at Kelly AFB, Texas, OC No 55 Sqn, Wg Cdr David Williams, was surprised to receive a signal from Ops Officer Pete Jackson bearing the recall codeword 'White Cliffs'. Saddam Hussein had invaded Kuwait, and after double-staging back though Gander, the Victor tankers landed back at Marham on the night of 9 August.

Two days later they refuelled Tornado F 3 air defence fighters through French airspace and over the Mediterranean. The Victors uplifted fuel at Nice and then flew back to Marham. They carried on with such towlines for quite some time as fast jets were ferried out to the Middle East.

The Bahrain-based crew of a No 55 Sqn K 2 pose proudly with the tanker's scoreboard, which shows the number of 'pump' transfers it had done during *Desert Storm*. They are, from left to right, David Williams (OC No 55 Sqn/Nav Plotter), Tim Hatcher (Captain), John Ingham (AEO) and Tim Walker (co-pilot)

A view through the K 2 rear periscope of a US Navy F-14A from VF-33, embarked aboard the aircraft carrier USS *America* (CV-66), that has pitched up for vital replenishment. This aircraft is fulled armed with Sidewinder and Sparrow air-to-air missiles

On 25 September, one Victor gave so much fuel away that it could not get back to Akrotiri and had to divert into Cairo.

Up to the end of November 1990, VC10 tankers operating out of Bahrain supplied RAF aircraft in -theatre. Then the planners decided that the VC10s needed support, so four No 55 Sqn Victors were deployed there in mid-December. Their first task was to fly 'Hosam Lo' towlines, which took fast jets up towards the Iraqi border. The K 2s then flew racetracks awaiting their return. The Tornado crews knew where Victor racetracks were and they only broke radio silence crossing the border outbound. On 20 December one crew gave so much fuel away that it could not get back to Bahrain and had to land at Dharan, in Saudi Arabia. Different racetracks included 'Mango Lo' and 'Olive Lo'. Flying continued over Christmas Eve and Christmas Day.

More Victors came out in the New Year, and the campaign to free Kuwait started on 16 January 1991. At 2330hrs, No 55 Sqn Victors took off so that the first Muharraq-based Tornado GR 1s, loaded with JP233 airfield denial weapons, could be launched on bombing missions across the Iraq border at 0100 hrs when war was declared. The K 2s operated along the 'Olive Lo' trail, which ran south of the Iraqi border, before turning on to a short northerly leg and casting off the Tornados into the heart of enemy territory. Tanker crews walked out at 2300 hrs to their aircraft, which were all set to Combat Ready. 'As we walked across a pan that was heaving with aircraft, all you could smell was burnt aviation fuel and there was so much noise', recalled a K 2 pilot.

No 55 Sqn flew right the way through Operation *Desert Storm*, (known as Operation *Granby* to the RAF) seven days and nights per week. Wg Cdr Williams flew 34 sorties in XL161, XL164, XL190, XL231, XM672, XM715 and XM717. His last operation was on 27 February. While VC10s in Saudi Arabia replenished the air defenders, No 55 Sqn at Bahrain supported the strike Tornado GR 1s, Jaguar GR 1As and Buccaneer S 2Bs. The Jaguar GR 1As operated close to the Kuwaiti border, while longer ranging Tornado GR 1s went deep into Iraq supported by the laser-designating Buccaneer S 2Bs. There was no plan

The final paint scheme – a K 2 of No 57 Sqn in the 'low conspicuity' hemp finish (*Millard*)

to support US Navy jets (probe and drogue Victors could not refuel USAF aircraft), but none were turned away if they pitched up.

On most days and nights the squadron allocated four primary Victors plus two reserves. A crew could be a reserve during the day and fly at night. No 55 Sqn flew 299 sorties and did not miss one. Victors dispensed more then 8,000,000 lbs of fuel during the 42-day conflict, and there was only one accident when a K 2 hit a pole on a low loader on a crowded pan that took seven feet off the wing tip. A new wing tip was sent out from the UK and the tanker carried on.

The last Victor flight took place on 30 November 1993, and today two Victors remain in running condition at Bruntingthorpe and Elvington. The Victor's existence spanned 40 years from first prototype flight to final sortie. The crescent-winged Victor was years ahead of its time and it flew smoothly at altitude like a knife through butter. The Victor provided Britain with its highest flying and largest bomb-carrying nuclear warplane. It was a superb strategic reconnaissance asset, and in the twilight of its career the Victor did sterling service as an airborne tanker. The Victor was the last of the V-bombers to enter service and the last to retire 40 years later. Set against any criteria, that was a remarkable achievement for a remarkably flexible aeroplane. And if you look at the futuristic stealth shapes now being bandied about, some of them bear a remarkable similarity to the Handley Page Victor.

This Victor K 2 formation was put up by No 55 Sqn for its disbandment flypast in October 1993 (*Gardner*)

APPENDICES

VICTOR SQUADRONS

No 232 OCU – B Flt of No 232 OCU was formed at Gaydon on 28 November 1957 to train Victor B 1/1A crews. C Flt duly received its first B 2s on 1 November 1961 at Cottesmore, after which it moved to Wittering to become the Victor B 2 Training Flight until 1968. B Flt remained at Gaydon, however, training Victor B 1/1A crews until No 232 OCU disbanded on 30 June 1965. The following day, the Tanker Training Flight stood-up at Marham. No 232 OCU reformed at Marham on 6 June 1970 and disbanded on 4 April 1986 (stylised probe and drogue insignia).

No 10 Sqn – Formed at Cottesmore on 15 April 1958 with the Victor B 1. The unit disbanded on 1 March 1964 (winged arrow insignia).

No 15 Sqn – Formed at Cottesmore on 1 September 1958 with the Victor B 1/1A. The unit disbanded on 1 October 1964 (hind's head insignia).

No 55 Sqn – Formed at Honington on 1 September 1960 with the Victor B 1/1A. The squadron moved to Marham on 24 May 1965, where it subsequently operated the Victor B(K) 1A, K 1A, K 1 and finally the K 2. The unit disbanded on 15 October 1993 (cubit arm grasping spear insignia).

No 57 Sqn – Formed at Honington on 1 January 1959 with the Victor B 1/1A. The squadron was transferred to Marham on 1 December 1965 and subsequently flew the Victor K 1, K 1A and K 2 prior to being disbanded on 30 June 1986 (phoenix rising from logs insignia or stylised red 57 in white disc).

No 100 Sqn – Formed at Wittering on 1 May 1962 and equipped with the Victor B 2/2R. The unit disbanded on 30 September 1968 (skull and crossbones insignia).

No 139 Sqn – Formed at Wittering on 1 February 1962 and equipped with the Victor B 2/2R. The unit disbanded on 31 December 1968 (fasces in front of crescent moon insignia).

No 214 Sqn – Formed at Marham on 1 July 1966 and equipped with the Victor K 1/1A. The squadron was disbanded on 28 January 1977 (nightjar in flight insignia).

No 543 Sqn – Formed at Wyton in May 1965 with the Victor B(SR) 2. The unit disbanded on 24 May 1974 (crane with open padlock in its beak (insignia).

1
Victor B 1 XA917 of the A&AEE, RAF Boscombe Down, 1956
XA917 was the first production Victor B 1, being delivered in the standard RAF lightweight matt aluminium finish. It served as a trials aircraft until dismantled after a crash-landing at Radlett in January 1964, whereupon the nose went to Marham to be used as a crew drill trainer.

2
Victor B 1 XA931 of No 232 OCU, RAF Gaydon, 1958
XA931 was the first Victor to enter operational squadron service, being issued to No 232 OCU in November 1957. It remained with the unit until December 1961, when XA931 moved to No 10 Sqn at Cottesmore. The bomber went back to No 232 OCU in August 1963, before being retired to the V-bomber Maintenance Unit at St Athan, near Cardiff. It was broken up in April 1974. XA931 was the first Victor to be finished in the all-white anti-flash Titanine paint scheme.

3
Victor B 1 XA940 of No 10 Sqn, RAF Cottesmore, 1958
XA940 served with No 10 Sqn (note the unit's winged arrow badge on the fin) until its undercarriage failed to lock down on 19 December 1961. After being repaired, the bomber subsequently served with No 232 OCU and then Nos 10 and 15 Sqn, before being transferred to the Honington Wing and No 57 Sqn in March 1965. XA940 moved to the Tanker Training Flight at Marham in January 1967 and thence to St Athan as an instructional airframe in July 1968.

4
Victor B 1 XH588 of No 15 Sqn, RAF Cottesmore, 1959
XH588 joined No 15 Sqn on 30 October 1958 and soon sported the unit's XV marking on its fin. The bomber was converted into a B 1A in August 1961 before moving to No 55 Sqn at Honington. XH558 returned to Handley Page for conversion into a K 1A tanker in 1966, after which it served successively with Nos 214, 55 and 57 Sqns at Marham. It was retired to Machrihanish for fire fighting training on 30 July 1975.

5
Victor B 1A XH619 of No 57 Sqn, RAF Honington, 1961
XH619, in low conspicuity white finish with a phoenix badge on the fin, joined No 57 Sqn as a B1 on 25 June 1959 before being converted to a B 1A in 1961. The B 1A was most recognisable by its rounded tail cone housing the tail-warning radar. XH619 stayed with the Honington Wing until the end of 1965, when it was converted into a K 1A tanker. Thereafter it served with Nos 55 and 214 Sqns at Marham before being retired to the base fire dump on 30 June 1975.

6
Victor B 2 XH668 of the A&AEE, RAF Boscombe Down, 1959
XH668, the first production Victor B 2 which retained the B 1 fin root, was delivered to the RAF on 3 June 1959. On 20 August XH668 crashed off Pembrokeshire during high speed trials when the starboard pitot tube fell away, causing the aircraft to break up in an uncontrollable high speed dive.

7
Victor B 2 XH669 of the A&AEE, RAF Boscombe Down, 1960
XH669 arrived at Boscombe Down on 22 December 1959 with a new fin root to house the intakes providing ram air for cooling the rear ECM gear and for anti-icing. It went back to Handley Page for conversion into a B 2R before joining the Wittering Wing on 8 July 1964. The aircraft was converted into a K 2 tanker prior to joining No 57 Sqn at Marham on 20 January 1977. XH669 broke its probe during 'Black Buck 1' on 1 May 1982. The aircraft served with No 55 Sqn from March 1986 until 21 June 1990, when it suffered an inflight fire. The aircraft was not repaired and XH669 was passed on to the Waddington fire section. Scrapped on 12 May 1995 by Hanninfield Metals of Stock, in Essex, the aircraft's cockpit section was preserved by Nigel Towler's Cockpit Collection at Southend airport, also in Essex.

8
Victor B 2R XL158 of No 139 Sqn, RAF Wittering, 1963
XL158 was delivered as a B 2 to the RAF at the end of 1960. It was retrofitted to B 2R standard on 1 June 1962 and issued to No 139 Sqn on 27 September 1963. The gloss white finish with pale blue and pink markings and pale blue serial numbers is completed by the unit's fasces and crescent crest on the tail. The B 2R had an extended ECM fit, with six peripheral aerials around the Red Steer antenna on the tail cone. The air intake for cooling all these ECM devices was positioned in the new fin leading edge extension. After conversion into a K 2, XL158 joined No 55 Sqn at Marham on 12 April 1976. The aircraft was scrapped at Marham in December 1993.

9
Victor B 2R XM718 of No 100 Sqn, RAF Wittering, 1963
XM718, sporting the No 100 Sqn 'skull and crossbones' crest on its fin, was the last Victor to roll off the production line. It joined No 100 Sqn on 2 May 1963, but the aircraft suffered a heavy landing when the tail parachute was inadvertently

deployed on the Wittering approach. While undergoing repair XM718 was partially converted into a B 2R (the Blue Steel control panel was retained). It joined No 543 Sqn at Wyton on 3 January 1966 and moved to No 232 OCU at Marham on 24 September 1974. The aircraft was scrapped on 3 March 1976.

10

Victor B 2R XH675 of No 100 Sqn, RAF Wittering, 1964

XH675, seen here in all-white finish with an underslung Blue Steel missile, lacks its full ECM aerial fit in this profile. The aircraft left Wittering in October 1968 and joined No 55 Sqn at Marham as a K 2 tanker on 30 March 1977. It moved to No 55 Sqn on 1 October 1980 and was scrapped in December 1993.

11

Victor B 2R XL513 of the Wittering Wing, RAF Wittering, 1965

XL513 was the first Victor to be painted by Handley Page at Radlett in the low-level, glossy polyurethane camouflage of dark green and medium sea grey, with serial numbers in white. Joining No 139 Sqn at Wittering in December 1963, the aircraft experienced an undercarriage failure at Manston on 8 January 1968 while still serving with the unit. Following conversion into a K 2 tanker, it joined No 55 Sqn at Marham on 21 March 1975. XL513 was written off following a birdstrike departing Marham on 28 September 1976. The pilot abandoned the take-off and overshot the end of the runway, at which point the aircraft caught fire and was destroyed. The crew escaped the Victor unscathed.

12

Victor B 2R XL192 of the Wittering Wing, RAF Wittering, 1966

XL192 joined No 100 Sqn on 28 June 1962. The cabin door blew off in flight on 22 March 1963 and it went back to Radlett for retrofitting to B 2R standard in January 1964. The aircraft returned to the Wittering Wing on 23 November 1964, as shown by the lion badge on fin. To minimise detection at low-level, the bomber's serials have been reapplied in black. XL192 was converted into a K 2 tanker and joined No 57 Sqn at Marham on 16 June 1976. It moved across to No 55 Sqn on 1 July 1986 and it was eventually struck off service for spares recovery on 7 July 1988.

13

Victor B 1A XH667 of the Honington Wing, RAF Honington, 1964

XH667 was the last Victor B 1 to roll off the Radlett production line on 31 March 1960. It was retained for conversion to B 1A standard before joining No 57 Sqn on 3 February 1961. By 1964 the Victor force had been resprayed in camouflage colours better suited to the aircraft's low-level nuclear penetration mission. XH667 was withdrawn for

conversion into a K 1A (K 2P) tanker on 11 February 1965, and it joined No 55 Sqn at Marham on 27 May 1965. The aircraft moved to No 214 Sqn on 1 April 1967 and it was retired to the Hal Far fire dump in Malta on 23 September 1975.

14

Victor B(SR) 2 XH672 of No 543 Sqn, RAF Wyton, 1969

XH672 rolled off the production line on 26 May 1960. After service as a trials aircraft, it was converted into an SR 2 and delivered to No 543 Sqn at Wyton on 13 August 1965 – the squadron crest of a crane with an open lock in its bill is superimposed on the tail. The shield on the nose bears the insignia of Nos 51, 58 and 543 Sqns, all of which were based at Wyton – the home of the RAF's aerial reconnaissance units at that time. XH672 was converted into a K 2 tanker in March 1974 before joining No 57 Sqn and then No 55 Sqn at Marham. On 30 November 1993 the Victor was flown to Shawbury, where it was dismantled for transportation to Cosford. In 2007, after more than a decade of being displayed in the open, XH672 became a key feature of the National Cold War Exhibition within the RAF Museum Cosford.

15

Victor B 1 XA930 of the A&AEE, RAF Boscombe Down, 1961

XA930 was delivered to the RAF on 30 September 1957, and it is depicted here in all-white, with a trial fit nose probe and underwing tanks. Having spent much of its early career conducting trials flights with the A&AEE and Handley Page, the aircraft subsequently joined No 10 Sqn on 30 September 1963, before moving to No 232 OCU and then the Honington Wing on 18 March 1965. Converted into a K 1 prior to being assigned to No 55 Sqn at Marham on 3 April 1967, XA930 moved across to No 214 Sqn on 1 August 1967 and was eventually retired to St Athan on 9 July 1974.

16

Victor B(K) 1A XH620 of No 55 Sqn, RAF Marham, 1965

XH620 served with No 57 Sqn before being converted into a B 1A in April 1961. It later became the first BK 1A interim tanker, and the aircraft is seen here after it had joined No 55 Sqn at Marham on 21 May 1965. Over the following ten years the Victor alternated between the TTF, No 57 Sqn, No 232 OCU and No 55 Sqn, before being struck off charge at St Athan on 24 June 1976.

17

Victor K 1 XA937 of No 214 Sqn, RAF Marham, 1966

XA937 joined No 10 Sqn as a B 1 bomber on 4 June 1958. It later became the first Victor to be converted into a K 1, whereupon it went to No 57 Sqn at Marham on 15 February 1966. The aircraft moved across to No 214 Sqn on 3 October 1966, and it seen here with the unit's distinctive nightjar in flight insignia on its fin. XA937 retired to St Athan on 7 February 1977.

18
Victor K 1A XH618 of No 57 Sqn, RAF Marham, 1967
XH618 joined No 15 Sqn on 15 August 1960 after conversion into a B 1A. It undertook Victor low-level trials in 1963, prior to conversion into a K 1A. The aircraft joined No 57 Sqn at Marham on 15 August 1966, the unit's '57' insignia being clearly visible on the fin. On 24 March 1975, a Buccaneer taking part in simulated refuelling struck the tailplane of XH618, bunting the tanker over and making it impossible for the rearcrew to escape. The captain managed to reach the ejection handle with the fingers of one hand, and although injured, he was subsequently rescued by a merchant ship. XH618 exploded as it reached the cloud tops.

19
Victor B 1A XH592 of the Tanker Training Flight, RAF Marham, 1968
XH592 joined No 15 Sqn on 2 February 1959 and went for conversion to B 1A standard on 1 September 1961. It was sent to the Honington Wing on 5 July 1962 and No 232 OCU on 11 March 1965. Although XH592 was never converted into a tanker, it served on the TTF at Marham from 23 June 1965 as a conversion trainer – TTF markings are clearly visible on the Victor's fin. XH592 remained on the TTF and then No 232 OCU until it was retired to the technical training school at Cosford on 16 October 1974. Sold for scrap after spending a number of years stored at St Athan, the aircraft's nose was saved by Phoenix Aviation of Bruntingthorpe aerodrome. When purchased it was in a poor state, with the underfloor area having suffered particularly badly from moisture and the attentions of various wildlife. All panelling in this area had since been replaced by Phoenix Aviation to stop any further infiltration. The cockpit interior is generally complete towards the front, but restoration continues on the rear crew area.

20
Victor B(SR) 2 XL193 of No 543 Sqn, RAF Wyton, 1970
XL193 joined No 100 Sqn at Wittering as a B 2 bomber on 30 August 1962. It was returned to Handley Page's Radlett plant for conversion into an SR 2 on 17 August 1964, whereupon it was sent to No 543 Sqn at Wyton on 21 June 1966. The aircraft is shown here with later B type roundels and fin flash plus sampling devices fitted to the underwing tanks for 'sniffing' the atmosphere after nuclear tests in the Pacific. XL193 was subsequently retired to St Athan on 3 April 1975.

21
Victor K 2 XL233 of No 232 OCU, RAF Marham, 1974
XL233 started life as a trials aircraft before being converted into a B 2R for delivery to the Wittering Wing on 10 April 1964. It was the first K 2 to enter RAF service when it arrived at Marham on 8 May 1974. Seen here in standard camouflage, XL233 served with No 232 OCU until 1 January 1977, when it moved across to No 55 Sqn. The aircraft was retired to St Athan on 31 July 1986.

22
Victor K 2 XL190 of No 55 Sqn, RAF Marham, 1982
XL190 joined No 139 Sqn as a B 2 bomber on 3 May 1962. It was converted into a B 2R and returned to the Wittering Wing on 28 April 1964. After conversion into a K 2 tanker, the aircraft joined No 232 OCU on 12 December 1974. It moved to No 55 Sqn on 8 December 1975, and here it sports a locally applied sharksmouth that appeared on the aircraft at Ascension Island shortly after the Falklands campaign. It was the first K 2 to be resprayed in the 'low conspicuity' hemp finish, this scheme being applied during an overhaul at Marham in the spring of 1982. This scheduled maintenance period meant that XL190 was the only Victor not to play a part in the war effort. After a short time with No 57 Sqn in 1984, XL190 returned to No 55 Sqn, where it remained until retirement on 19 October 1992.

23
Victor K 2 XL160 of No 57 Sqn, RAF Marham, 1984
XL160, here in 'low conspicuity' hemp finish with No 57 Sqn's phoenix badge and LVII on fin, served as a B 2R with the Wittering Wing before moving to No 55 Sqn at Marham after K 2 conversion on 22 September 1975. It moved to No 57 Sqn on 2 October 1980 and back to No 55 Sqn on 12 August 1985. The aircraft rejoined No 57 Sqn in January 1986 and was retired on 2 July that same year.

24
Victor K 2 XM717 of No 55 Sqn, RAF Marham, 1992
XM717 was delivered to No 100 Sqn on 14 March 1963. After conversion into a B 2R, it returned to the Wittering Wing on 2 February 1965. The aircraft joined No 543 Sqn at Wyton on 7 January 1969 and was converted to K 2 standard before assigment to No 55 Sqn on 1 November 1977. It is shown here with nose art and No 55 Sqn's 'arm with spear' crest during Operation *Granby*. The K 2 was retired on 1 October 1993 and its nose is presently displayed in the RAF Hendon Museum.

BIBLIOGRAPHY

Brookes, Andrew, *The V-force - The History of Britain's Airborne Deterrent*, Jane's, 1982

Jefford, C G, *RAF Squadrons*, Airlife, 2001

Wynn, Humphrey, *RAF Nuclear Deterrent Forces*, HMSO, 1994

INDEX

Page numbers in **bold** denote illustrations. Brackets show captions to colour plates.